Rugby Generations

by
Jos Andrews

With a foreword by Nigel Owens

Published by Accent Press Ltd 2016

ISBN 9781786150127

This book was produced using funding from the Welsh Books Council

Printed in Great Britain

To Geraint Evans, who really knows and loves rugby, and to my dad, Ronald Andrews, who never missed an opportunity to play and watch sport.

CONTENTS

AUTHOR'S NOTE

What makes rugby great? The players.

We shout for them, we cheer and applaud them. We cry for them. Their stories are universal. The generations may be different but the underlying sense of pride in team and country never changes.

It has been a pleasure and a privilege to spend time with some of the greats of the game.

I should add that none of the chapter contributors had any idea that I was going to invite other great sportsmen and rugby players to write their introductions. I hope these come as a well-deserved surprise to them all.

FOREWORD

By Nigel Owens
International Rugby Union Referee

The first recollection I have of my love for rugby union was the Scotland v Wales game at Murrayfield in 1977. As a six-year-old, I watched the match on television with my dad and I can still hear Bill McLaren's voice as he described a fantastic Phil Bennett try. The move had been started by Gerald Davies, carried on by David Burcher and Steve Fenwick for Phil Bennett to dummy and sidestep his way under the posts. 'This is going to be the try of the Championship,' said McLaren, as Phil put the brown rugby match ball down and rested it under his chin for what seemed like an age.

After the game, I couldn't wait to go out into the fields behind my house in Mynydd Cerrig with my own brown rugby ball, pretending to be Phil Bennett. That moment on TV sealed it for me; I was hooked on rugby football!

Some years later, my dad and a couple of family friends began taking me to watch Tumble in all their home and away games. They were a great side in those days, winning everything in West Wales – it seemed to me – including the much-prized Tovali Cup. Tumble rugby club meant such a lot to my family and me and, as an added bonus, my first cousin Phil Owens played for the team as well.

Another episode that endeared me to this great game was during a Welsh Youth International in Whitland. Eryl Price, the Tumble Youth hooker, was winning his first cap and so, quite naturally, my dad, my uncle and I went to support him. Some two rows back in the stand was the late, great Ray Gravell, who, having retired from playing the game, was now working for Radio Cymru. Dad said, 'Look who's behind you!' I turned around and Grav gave me a thumbs up and said hello. One of the legends who I had been watching and cheering on television for years was sitting in the stand behind me and, more than that, had acknowledged me in his own inimitable way.

FOREWORD: NIGEL OWENS

These things were what made rugby so special for me and made me want to be part of the game.

I wish I could say that I went on to emulate my heroes by having played the game to a high standard – but I can't. As a pupil at Maes Yr Yrfa, I was fortunate to be in the school team. It didn't have many pupils and, as my friend Craig Bonnell was the captain of the rugby team, my chances of selection were improved no end.

We were not the most successful of school teams and had failed, one particular season, to win a single match. Against Ysgol Gruffydd Jones from St Clears, we had managed a late try under the posts to bring the scores level at 12-12. Playing full back that day, I told my captain I was going to take the conversion, anticipating what a school hero I would be if I kicked the winning points – our first victory of the season. My conversion sadly went nearer the corner flag than the uprights, which resulted in two things: Craig, my friend and captain, didn't speak to me for a fortnight and the late John Beynon, my games master, suggested I take up refereeing!

To me, rugby football is the greatest game of all. You play hard, but you play fair. You take it seriously, but it can be great fun as well, and friends made on the field of play can last you a lifetime. Rugby instils in you the importance of respect. You learn, as a young child, not only the laws of the game, but to respect your own team, the opposition and the referee. These things are vital in the continued development of the game, and place a huge responsibility on those involved in teaching and coaching to maintain those core values.

I have been fortunate in that I have been involved in international rugby at the highest level, but, when time permits, I still try to put something back at junior and grassroots level. That's where it all starts for me. The rugby club is a huge part of the community and none of the international players or referees like myself would be where we are today if it weren't for those rugby-loving communities. Rugby has helped me to succeed in everything I have done and to be the person I am. It has been the constant friend in good and troubled times. I owe much more to this wonderful game than the game will ever owe me.

Rugby union, like everything else, will inevitably develop and change in the future as new ideas are incorporated and accepted. Many of those will be for the good of the game but, in the process

FOREWORD: NIGEL OWENS

of changing, I hope that the well-established values of respect and fair play will remain. A proper balance must be struck between, on the one hand, embracing change and, on the other, maintaining the game's very best traditions. We owe that to our future generations.

CHAPTER ONE

Introduction by Gerald Davies
Cambridge University, Llanelli RFC, Cardiff RFC, London Welsh, Barbarians, Wales, British and Irish Lions

As a youngster, growing up in Llansaint, I practised my rugby skills in the open field of Parc-Y-Ty overlooking Cefn Sidan and Carmarthen Bay. For a schoolboy who dared to dream, that field was reshaped in the mind's eye to become the lush green playing surface of any number of rugby's most iconic stadiums. It was the home, always, of free-flowing, glorious rugby and my team proved, imaginatively, time and time again, to be the scourge of visiting touring teams.

For a while though, I contented myself with dummying and sidestepping cowslips and cowpats, but all the time I wanted to be like ... well, who? The dream crystallised when I went to Stradey Park,

Llanelli one mid-week evening straight from school and saw DK (Ken) Jones in action for the Scarlets against the Irish Wolfhounds. With his flowing blond hair, sculptured physique and pace to burn, DK was the player I wanted to be, and from the highly populated – but often judgemental – Tanner Bank, we rose as one to salute a great DK try.

He ran from inside his own half, sidestepping three people – oh, at least three – in quick succession, with style, elegance and a razor-like cutting edge to dive spectacularly across the line under the posts. The game was not for the physique of the bully, it allowed for artistic expression: clever and smart, pleasing to the eye and chasing for glory.

There were other occasions, other tries, like the one for the British Lions against the Springboks at Ellis Park, Johannesburg in 1962 – thankfully recorded on film for posterity. The try at Stradey, however, is my one glowing, inspiring memory of DK's irrepressible and irresistible style. What a rugby legend! What a role model! He was the kind of rugby player I wanted to be.

DK Jones

*Oxford University, Llanelli RFC, Cardiff RFC,
Barbarians, Wales and the British and Irish Lions*

No one in my family had ever played rugby, but I was brought up in a village – Cross Hands – where rugby was a way of life.

I was good at sport from a very early age, though no one else in my family was. If in doubt, the family always knew where they could find me … kicking a ball outside in the fields. My other great love was snooker and, from the age of ten until about fifteen years of age, I spent as much of my free time as I could in the Working Man's Hall in Cross Hands. All of the local boys would congregate there from ten o'clock in the morning until six or seven o'clock at night. My mother would have to leave what she was doing to come out and bring me home for my lunch or supper, as I would have lost track of time completely, immersed in game after game. My friends and I would spend all day chatting around the three large, oak snooker tables, setting up knockout competitions, each of us determined to be the best player in the village.

There was nothing else to occupy us as the weather always seemed awful and there were no other facilities for us to enjoy. The hall was our salvation, an arena where we were kings of the sport. The other great joy was sliding down the huge, black coal tips surrounding the village, on an old zinc sheet with the front bent upwards to form a sledge shape, imagining we were sliding down huge mountains of snow! The tips were twice the size of a large house and we'd whizz down, oblivious to the danger. No amount of warnings from the family were heeded. They were great times; we were carefree, and happy with the little we had. There was no money about, so we made our own fun with whatever was to hand. I was never injured – though more by luck than skill or judgement!

From the age of fifteen I began to realise the importance of school studies. My parents wanted me to understand that without an education the coal mine was the only alternative and they wanted more for me. At school, I worked hard, but sport was always foremost in my mind. I excelled at athletics and rugby and my teachers at Gwendraeth Grammar School encouraged and guided me to play well. They could see, as local clubs did, that I had a talent and a passion for the game.

I had great sports masters at Gwendraeth School:

Wil Erith and Ray Williams – devoted and committed teachers who'd stay behind after school taking time to teach us how to sprint, how to pass and how to kick. They were marvellous role models and taught us how to behave on and off the field. They took a great interest in their pupils, staying behind in the nights and at weekends to pass on their knowledge of the game. They cared about their subject and loved rugby. Ray Williams was an excellent rugby player himself, a first class Llanelli and Wales winger. They would arrange for us to play the local grammar schools – Whitland, Pembroke Dock, Ardwyn, Carmarthen, Ammanford, Llanelli, Gower, Llandeilo – quietly demonstrative when we won. I loved sport in school from an early age because of these teachers, and was proud to be made captain of the school under-19s rugby team.

As a boy, I also played for the local schoolboys' side, Mynydd Mawr, in the Dewar Shield competition. I was noticed, and I gained an under-15 schoolboys' cap against Scotland in Cardiff Arms Park, and a second one against England in Bristol in 1956. I played fly half in my school games usually, but I was chosen to play full back for those two games. It wasn't my usual position, but I just got on with it, pleased to play in any position! Cyril Davies, who was a little ahead of me in school, was a brilliant centre who had a Welsh cap. He was an outstanding secondary school player with a wonderful burst of speed and change of pace. I really admired him, could see how good he was and wanted to emulate that. He was an exceptionally talented player and never really had the recognition he deserved, I felt. Schools rugby was very important in those days and was the nursery for so many great Welsh international players.

My father was a miner in the Gwendraeth Valley. He was a strong socialist. We spoke Welsh at home as a family and chapel was very important with three visits on a Sunday. My father had never followed Llanelli, the local first-class team, but he began to take an interest as he could see how important the sport was to me. He realised, like my teachers and coaches, that I had something special and was proud that people had begun to notice my prowess. I was always fast on the field, as I did a lot of sprinting and athletics in the summer months. I could run a hundred yards in ten seconds and that speed gave me a real advantage over my opponents on the rugby pitch.

My father's job meant that we didn't have money to go on holidays. Holidays for me were staying with my aunts for two or three days in different local villages – Pontyberem, Pontiets, Drefach or Llanddarog. We never went abroad or away on a family holiday. Rugby gave me the chance to travel, which was amazing to me. My first trip abroad was at the age of sixteen when we went to play the French schoolboys under-19s in Cognac. To meet people in another part of the world was unbelievable to me and my family at the time. We flew to Bordeaux and were taken by the French school for a visit around a brandy distillery and I couldn't wait to tell my parents all about it as it was so very different to what we knew at home. The fact that we won there made everything better too!

Travel gave me a huge incentive to play rugby well. To be able to visit other countries and meet new people was something I wanted to continue throughout my life. Rugby was a wonderful learning experience for me, and the tales that I related delighted my brother and sisters who were thrilled by my success.

I was aware of the sacrifices that my mother had to make for me to play rugby. She had to buy my boots, shorts and socks which were all extra expenses for the family budget. She never complained about all the extra washing and she would boil and starch my white shorts after each game. Often I'd have to fight to get into them – they were like aluminium pantaloons! She had no washing machine so everything was done by hand and then, in the first tackle of the game, I'd be straight in the mud and would ruin all her hard work! It was a hard life for housewives. Dad would come home filthy from the pit and Mam would be boiling water for him to wash in a big zinc tub at home. There were no pit baths until much later in his life.

Catherine Irene Gibbard, my mother, was a wonderful mam, an absolute queen! With four children she would be washing and cooking all day and she never sat down. There would always be a meal ready for my father to come home to, with everything cooked from scratch. He had been in a two-foot-ten-inch seam, lying on his back hacking coal out in the darkness all shift, and food at the end of the day was important. There was no pit canteen or pit toilet at that time. This was his life from 6 a.m. to 2 p.m. every day. I never thought of it as a youngster, but I realise now that my mother never knew if he would come home. As children, we had no idea of the fear she had, like all of the other miners' wives. We never thought of the dangers all the men of the village faced. No wonder he had no time to think about sport, his world was one of hard work. Yet no matter how tired he was, my father would come and watch me play for the school and he would appear at rugby trials to show support for his son.

I was thrilled to be made captain of the Welsh Secondary Schools, notified by Idris Cleaver, a schoolmaster at Pembroke Dock Grammar School who was the chairman of the secondary school selectors. Nothing like that had happened to the family before and they were delighted for me to be given the honour. I felt no pressure or fear; I just remember sheer pleasure. We didn't have a car, so it wasn't easy for my parents to come to see me play – transportation at that time and in that area was a problem. Also, they had four children and they wanted to be fair to us all.

* * *

I began playing for Llanelli RFC at the age of seventeen in my school holidays. My first game for the Scarlets was against the Universities Athletics Union on Christmas morning. They were on tour and so played against Swansea, Llanelli and Newport. It was an open and lively game as the university boys were fit and wanted to play entertaining rugby and we, in turn, responded. My family couldn't come to watch me as there was no public transport on Christmas Day. Kick-off was at eleven o'clock and my mother even delayed Christmas lunch for the family until I got back. Life was good! I was given the occasional game to nurture me slowly into senior rugby with games against clubs like Northampton, Halifax and Nuneaton.

Llanelli was a lovely club and so welcoming to players and supporters. Playing at such a young age amongst my local heroes was particularly special. I looked up to Cyril Davies and, of course, the great Carwyn James, a former pupil of Gwendraeth and a very talented player indeed. He was always special, a very clever, intelligent player who could read the game extremely well. He was skilful and would give advice on how to take care of yourself on the field against older and bigger opponents. I was given a lot of encouragement and advice by more seasoned players, which I will always be grateful for.

The president of the club, John Thomas, was a local businessman and he and Handel Greville were both very kind and good men. The secretary, Arthur Davies, was a local schoolmaster who understood the area and the people. They all took time and did their best for a club that meant the world to them.

My close friends in the Llanelli team were: Brian Davies, my co-centre, who had played for the secondary schools with me; Wyn Oliver who had played for Llanelli Grammar; and Terry Davies, another friend, who played at full back. It was a very happy time, with great team spirit making training and playing together a joy. Life revolves around personalities and Llanelli was full of wonderful characters at that time. Older players like Howard Davies, Brian Thomas, Aubrey Gale and Marsden Morgan were people you looked up to and wanted to be like. They were older, wiser and they looked after you. They took you under their wing, giving advice and protecting you on the field. Rugby is a tough, hard game and I remember them for the way they handled themselves on the field and how they watched out for us and taught us well. It was a privilege to learn from greats like this.

Rugby in Llanelli was a religion and a culture, and Stradey Park was the cathedral of rugby, a wonderful club to start my first class rugby career. There was a packed house every weekend, with fifteen thousand supporters turning up every Saturday. The London Welsh Boxing Day match would be full to capacity with eighteen to twenty thousand people turning up to cheer their team. They voted with their feet, turning up to a club that was the heart of the community; all roads led to Stradey on a Saturday afternoon. The game was simple then: everyone wore black boots, all our jerseys had a collar, there were no names as promotion on the jerseys – the focus was rugby. There were no pre-match events with flares and music at that time. There was no television coverage; you saw the game or you missed it! Kick-off was always 2.15 p.m. on a Saturday afternoon, as everyone knew.

* * *

I gained a place at Cardiff University to study Chemistry and Biochemistry and was still playing for Llanelli every Saturday for no payment. I came back at the weekends for the game, either by train to Swansea then a bus to Cross Hands or, when I was lucky enough, getting a lift with a teacher, Brian Thomas, who taught PE in Penarth Grammar and played second row for Llanelli. I was the only one in the family to go to university and my parents were thrilled. I received a grant, which made it possible, as my parents would have been unable to support me throughout my degree. I found myself jobs, either in hotels in Tenby as a kitchen porter or labouring on building sites. The seven to eight weeks' work in the holidays gave me a good wage and was helpful, so that I, in my turn, could give something back to my parents.

Life was about to get better. One day, a large, shiny, and very expensive Rolls Royce appeared in our village and stopped outside my home. I had a holiday job with Hubert Williams and Co of Burry Port, working on the building sites in Pontyberem, and arrived home to a sight that was the talk of the village! Curtains were twitching and the neighbours were out in force to see the splendid car and its occupants. My mother had made our guests tea and sandwiches and they were inside waiting to talk to me. It was a huge honour to be introduced to two officials from Leeds who invited me to come and play for their famous rugby league club. They were perfect gentlemen who didn't pressure me, but who offered a huge sum of money and a place at Leeds University to continue my studies if I signed with them. It was such a large sum that it was important to consider the offer very seriously. It was a big temptation and not one to turn down lightly.

My father sat, silent and thoughtful, as they spoke to us. He worked long, hard hours as a miner underground and the fee they offered was way beyond what he might ever earn. Living in a council house as we did, it would have been easy for him to suggest that

I should take the offer. That kind of money would have bought three or four houses for us at the time. To his credit, he simply said quietly, 'It's up to you.' He didn't try to influence me in any way and I look back with pride at the way he only wanted the best for me, when the money would have been very welcome for the family. He taught me a very important lesson: to be your own man. I decided against their offer, as I knew I wanted to keep control of my future career and not turn professional at that time just for the money. I felt there was more to life than being tied to a professional club at this stage. I wanted to travel and to be selected for my country. I realised then how great a man my father was that he let me make my own decision. Money has never swayed me and I hope it never will influence me to change my beliefs. I realised that money could change you and I never wanted to be bought. My dad had shown me a very strong and honourable way to live his life, and I hope I learnt that from him and always followed his example.

* * *

My first game for Wales was against England in Twickenham in 1962 at the age of twenty, while at Cardiff University. I couldn't have had a better first cap than against England. It was a great baptism. Bill Clements, the secretary of the Welsh Rugby Union, gave me my official letter with instructions for train travel arrangements to the game. Three of us selected for Wales, Dewi Bebb, Brian Davies and I, could all do a hundred yards in less than ten seconds – a fast trio for the team! We stayed in the Berners Hotel in London. The excitement of staying in a hotel and then having a police escort on the bus all the way from London to Twickenham was incredible. I thought I was the prime minister! To me, Twickenham seemed very strange: you never saw people having picnics in the car park of the Cardiff Arms Park, but here it seemed commonplace. Walking off the bus, I was amazed to see people eating from large, luxurious hampers placed in the boot of their cars; it was a different world – I'd never seen people eating and drinking wine and champagne in such style at a rugby match.

The atmosphere was fantastic as we entered the stadium, which was at full capacity of about sixty thousand at that time. The roaring and singing was deafening as we made our way inside. The dressing rooms were quite something too, with six or seven individual baths – unlike Llanelli where we had a very small communal bath, which we all washed in together after the game! We looked at each other, amazed at the luxury. We could see the huge class difference. The game in England was the product of the public schools whereas in Wales it was the working man's game. For us, the game was an escape from the mines, the quarries and the farms. It was a recreation from hard, physical, manual work.

The shirts were issued, with no great ceremony, by the 'masseur' (not called the physio in those days) in the changing room before the game. The team captain was scrum half, Lloyd H Williams, who gave his customary team talk fifteen minutes before kick-off. We ran out determined to play our best for him and for our country. The tradition of England versus Wales rivalry on the pitch was clear; there was no quarter given on the pitch in a hard physical battle, but immediately after the final whistle our opponents were delightful people to be with and great company. Both teams were driven to the Royal Garden Hotel in Kensington for the after-match dinner. It was a formal, black tie event with wonderful speeches delivered with banter instead of blows. Players like Michael Weston, the England centre, Dicky Jeeps the scrum half, Richard Sharp the fly half and Malcolm Phillips – later to be President of the RFU – were hard men on the pitch but great company afterwards. We might hit hell out of one another in the game, but once it was over everyone would be in the bar as friends. This aspect of the game is an important tradition for all involved.

* * *

My mother and father came to the match but, sadly, only two tickets were allocated per player and so none of my siblings could come. My parents had travelled to London to see that first game I played for Wales – a long journey of many hours then. The last time they had ventured to London had been for the Queen's Coronation in 1953. My father was incredibly proud to see me come out in the red jersey of Wales, to resounding cheers and applause at the Twickenham ground, the home of English rugby. He had gone to work in the mine at fourteen years of age and this was an experience beyond anything for him or my mother. He took a lot of ribbing in the local colliery on his return about his 'famous' son! Despite all the leg-pulling, all of his fellow miners were delighted for him and for me. My father was a very modest man who wasn't one to brag about his son's success, but I always knew how thrilled he was for me. On my return home, my mother had arranged a chicken dinner in the parlour with relatives and friends as a celebration. I knew how great an honour this was, as the parlour was sacrosanct and she had borrowed another table to give me a dinner to remember.

I played fourteen games for Wales as a centre; to represent my country was a huge honour for a proud Welshman. Being selected to join the British and Irish Lions tour in 1962 to South Africa at the age of twenty, as the only player from Llanelli, was a huge added bonus. Every player will tell you these are very special moments. I received a letter that began formally, 'Dear Jones ...' My parents were delighted – all the neighbours came to congratulate us! It created a huge stir in the village, as I was the first one from Cross Hands to go on a Lions tour. People were genuinely thrilled for me and for 'the patch'. The team was kitted out at the prestigious Lillywhites store in Piccadilly, London. It was a very different clothes shopping experience from the shops in Cross Hands! Each player was allocated two shirts, two blazers – a day blazer and an evening one – together with one pair of grey trousers, two ties and a British Lions dicky-bow tie for official functions. The team photo showed us all in our finery and there was a great deal of banter about who looked the best. I have to say that I thought we all looked very smart.

We must have looked good, as we were always given preference to board the plane. There was no business class, so we all piled into economy, to the astonishment of the other passengers faced by the entire British and Irish Lions making their way around the plane. The plane was a Comet 4, one of the postwar jets, and the world's first jet-propelled airliner. To travel on board something like this was in itself an adventure for most of us. No matter how tough we were on the rugby field, not everyone was so brave in the air!

We left London and refuelled in Rome. The actor Roger Moore was on the same flight and I remember people surrounding him, keen to talk to him as we sat in the VIP room. The press were there in force, poised with their cameras and notebooks as he was meeting someone who was to be his future wife, Luisa – a stunning dark-haired Italian lady. It was all a very glamorous, film-star world and very different from the one I was used to. We could only stare in amazement.

We then flew to Khartoum, the capital of Sudan, to refuel. As we landed, at one o'clock in the morning, and left the plane, I remember thinking that it was like walking into an oven and we looked at each other, thinking ahead to what playing rugby would be like in this kind of temperature. The airport was, at best, basic and we were delayed there for a few hours with the dust and heat blasting us from all directions. We then flew on to play in Nairobi, which was at the time very colonial as independence had not been granted yet and it was still under British rule.

We stayed two or three nights and flew on to Rhodesia where we stayed at the Meikles Hotel in the capital, Salisbury. It was a five star, sumptuous hotel with inconspicuous but instant service which impressed us all. We played two warm-up games, one on the Police Sports Ground in Salisbury and one in Bulawayo, the second largest city. They were good games as a pre-tour warm-up to settle us in to what awaited us in South African rugby.

Our hosts entertained us royally, taking us to see the grave of Cecil Rhodes, the former Prime Minister of the Cape Colony, and we also flew over the huge

Kariba Dam in Zambia. It truly was another world to us, seeing places that had previously only been names on a map. Our hosts took us to the tobacco sales and it was amazing to experience and understand the global power of cigarettes at that time. We were shown to a huge brokerage which sold tobacco worldwide, with all of the companies vying for the best price and quality. Cigarettes were still viewed as part of a film culture of glamour and style, with stars shown smoking on screen and in the newspapers, so there was a lot of money in the tobacco business.

We were invited by Sir Roy Welensky, the Prime Minister at the time, to a reception in Government House and were introduced to him formally, prior to the game, when he came to shake hands and offer a few words to us.

When we arrived in Johannesburg there was a huge reception, with thousands waiting for us at the airport. We felt like the Beatles with roaring crowds wherever we looked! We were completely astonished by the turnout. The wall of people and the deafening noise was something we weren't used to, but we were to learn quickly the importance placed on sport and the reputation of these Tests throughout South Africa. They took their sport seriously and were ready to take on the Lions.

Our team spirit was strong too. Commander Vaughan, the team manager, was a former Navy man who demanded high standards from his 'rugby recruits'. Spirits were high and we were welcomed warmly by a country that loves its rugby. After each game, we were presented with wonderful souvenirs of the tour: silver trays from Springs and Pretoria; cigarette and cigar boxes; wood carvings and Zulu spears and shields, which certainly proved interesting when carried home proudly on the plane. But apartheid was in clear view, with segregation in evidence all around us, and glaring poverty which was impossible to ignore. Jobs were allocated according to colour and this was evident wherever we played. It was very different to what we were used to at home.

We were away for four and a half months. I couldn't phone home as the cost was prohibitive and anyway we didn't have a phone at home. It was sad for me that it wasn't possible to tell my family immediately about all the amazing things we were doing and seeing. Letters were hugely important and the ceremonial giving out of the post from home was an important part of the week. The team all congregated together to find out who had letters and there was great happiness for those who received news, but also sadness if your post was delayed. This was our only line of communication with home and it meant the world. It was impossible to be homesick for long, though, as there was so much excitement and the tour was such an experience. In the evenings, we were invited to functions after each game

– to the British Ambassador's residence in Pretoria and to the different diplomatic consulates in Cape Town and Durban. In contrast, on the quiet nights the team were happy playing cards. All of the Lions were invited to have meals with local families and David Hewitt, the Irish centre, and I went to have Sunday lunch in Paarl after playing Boland on the Saturday. We made wonderful friendships from this and I have kept in touch with this family, Beyers and Annie Hugo, ever since, subsequently meeting their children – Louise, Marianne, and Linda – and their grandchildren, and hosting them and their families in Wales, which we continue to do.

* * *

In the first Test in Ellis Park, Johannesburg, a huge eighty-thousand-strong crowd greeted us as we ran out on the pitch and the roars were electrifying. This was the biggest crowd we had played in front of, and in such a fantastic stadium. They were determined to warn us what we might expect from their side when they emerged. South Africans are rightly proud of their rugby skills and we knew the games would be tough. I had played against South Africa in Stradey in 1960 when they were on tour and they always gave the impression of being bigger, stronger and more powerful. As someone said at the time, 'We were brought up on egg and chips … and they were brought up on steak and biltong!' They were huge, but very fit, athletic and mobile. I loved playing rugby there. The grounds were dry, the sun was on your back and you could run fast on top of the ground. The ball was always dry; we were used to playing in the thick mud of Cardiff Arms Park, expecting, and usually guaranteed to get, rain! To be able to play in such conditions and against such great opponents was a privilege. Johnny Gainsford was an excellent centre, Keith Oxlee an outstanding fly half, and Jannie Engelbrecht – the winger – an unbelievable player. Frik du Preez was someone I regarded as a superb player; he was, for me, a *complete* rugby player.

Our team was made of players from very different lifestyles. We were from all backgrounds and walks of life and that's what made the team blend so crucial. There were farmers, labourers, solicitors, students like myself, and stockbrokers, all sharing together and learning from each other. The unspoken but clear message was that we were all in this together and it was a powerful and important team ethos. Arthur Smith had captained Scotland before the British Lions. He was a former Scottish long jump champion and an excellent 400m runner with a first-class honours degree in mathematics and a PhD. On his international debut in 1955, the Scotland wing had ended his country's run of seventeen straight defeats with a spectacular try against Wales that saw the game go down in history as

---

'Arthur Smith's match'. The team talks then were just half an hour before kick-off, not planned over days of sessions. His message to us all was simple: Do your duty. There was no analysis of stats and figures, no re-runs of key moves. It was up to you to know your opposition players and analyse for yourself. It was for you to do your own thinking. It was you against another man, another team, and individual judgement was what made the team. Improvisation could turn a match and you had to do this on your own and trust your judgement.

* * *

It was unbelievably hot and the ground was rock hard, which suited my fast running game. Scrum half Dickie Jeeps, who was captain of England, was known by New Zealanders in 1959 as 'The India Rubber Man' for his brilliance with his ball passing skills from any angle. In 1962 in South Africa, they rated him highly too for his attacking skills and his marshalling of the pack. In that first game, he passed to Gordon Waddell, the Scottish fly half, who then passed to me and I raced seventy yards to score a try against our powerful opponents. I was thrilled to find out that it had been shown on the television news back at home so all of the village were able to celebrate with my family. My parents took it all in their stride, but they were still very proud of the number of people knocking doors to congratulate them. We drew 3-3. It was great to start the Test on a good note.

It was impossible not to be aware of the colonial regime everywhere we went. The ground was segregated and South Africa's racist sporting policies were evident. Black people sat together and were always put behind the goal posts. The Lions were always supported by the black community, who cheered loudly and sang songs whenever we were winning; they could not be silenced in their determination to show us we were the side they were rooting for.

It was an eye opener for me on that tour to be faced with the reality of apartheid and I felt very uneasy at what I was seeing. My uncle had been in the Navy during the war and, while he was in Cape Town, a local family of Cape Malay descent had looked after him. I was excited to meet them years later and obviously gave them tickets for the game, but they weren't allowed into the hotel with me. I was terribly upset, as they had treated my uncle so well, yet I was forced to meet them outside because of the colour of their skin. It was a cruel awakening to me. I loved South Africa – the country, the people I had met and its wide-open spaces and sun – but I didn't like what I saw of its social politics. The separation of people in the rugby grounds and outside horrified me. Separate buses, parks and restaurants were something I had never come across. I believed that you should treat everyone the same and I had been taught by my father to judge people on their own merits. My experiences there taught me a great deal.

My father was interested to find out what I had learnt of the miners in South Africa and whether they were like the miners of Wales. He would never be able to afford to visit the country but he was keen to hear my stories and enjoy his son's success through our chats. A trip was arranged by our hosts, the Transvaal Rugby Federation, to see the Durban Deep gold mine. We were taken ten thousand feet below ground and some of the players were quite frightened of going this far.

My father wanted to know the differences between the coal mines I knew from home and the gold mine I had been taken to see. I explained how much cleaner it was than the black dust he was so used to. Also, I told him of the intense heat the miners there had to endure. In the gold mines they extracted the gold and refined it on site. It was fantastic to see the end product of gold bars as the entire process was detailed before us. That was interesting for my father, who was fascinated to learn more of miners in another land. He was astonished to learn that every Sunday morning there was a tribal dance-off competition at the mines. A crowd always came to watch and support and the participants took the challenge very seriously. I found it interesting thinking of the miners' singing competitions at home in Wales.

Mining was an enormous industry for South Africa and my father wanted to know whether there was a fair wage for the workers. His sense of brotherhood and fairness, learnt underground, is something I have always tried to apply in rugby and in life.

We were disappointed to lose the series. The Test in Pretoria was the last game before coming back and we lost heavily, which was hard to take. It had been a long tour and we were glad by then to be returning home. My brother, Terry, met me at the airport and on the long drive home from London it was good to hear all of the news from the family and bring myself back to life in Wales. From living four months in top hotels, it was back to the council house in Cross Hands – and no grand celebration at home, it was back to earth! I was only too aware that I would never have been able to go to South Africa without rugby and, more than that, would never have met the people I had, or enjoyed the experiences I was offered through the game.

* * *

I had just finished my second year at Cardiff University and going back into the third year it was hard to settle down after being away for such a long time. I'd been living in a very artificial world, playing rugby and enjoying the good times. Now it was back to reality … and rain! It was hard to adjust to university life and study again, but I knew that my future depended on it, so I had to knuckle down to hard work. I was still playing at weekends for Llanelli. The club had been following the tour via stories in the *Western Mail*, *The Times*, the *Daily Mail* and the *Daily Herald*. There had only been about five reporters in all those months on the tour, so different to today where reporters, and television and radio crews, number an army who follow the matches.

* * *

During my third year at Cardiff, Onllwyn Brace, who played with me at Llanelli, suggested that I should apply to Oxford for my postgraduate year. He had also studied for three years in Cardiff before going up to Oxford. It was my first time seeing the city of dreaming spires; I felt in awe of it then and still feel that same awe each time I go back. My interview with the Professor of Education lasted about forty-five minutes and all the time I knew that I really wanted to be part of this great collegiate university. No one could fail to be impressed by the historical majesty of the buildings making up the oldest university in the English-speaking world. It was a life changing moment for me. I'm not ashamed to say that I felt a little inferior on arrival. Everywhere I turned, there seemed to be the great and the good from all around the world.

The greatest difficulty I had on receiving my letter of acceptance was to choose which of the colleges I would go to. The majority of Welsh people chose to go to Jesus College, but the captain of the Oxford rugby team at the time, Nick Silk (who later played for England), from Merton College, showed me around and I was so impressed that I applied there. I was looked after by my scout, Charlie, and his lovely wife, Mavis, from Aberdare. They looked after my room and were wonderful to me, though I was not in the same league as another they had looked after – JRR Tolkien. Their role was to look after all the students' requirements, tidying rooms and cleaning, but for me they were just delightful people who became great friends. Mavis called us 'her boys' and we were lucky to have her.

I ate nightly in the college dining hall at 7 p.m., dressed formally in *sub-fusc* which was mandatory. The food was superb and the atmosphere an event in itself. One of my fellow students on the Diploma of Education course was Jeffrey Archer, now Baron Archer, prolific writer and former Tory deputy chairman. He was a good athlete and I used to run against him on the Iffley Road track.

Having received an Oxford Blue, I was invited to become a member of the Vincent's Club, a renowned institution founded in 1863 in King Edward Street, a sporting club independent from the colleges. Members of the club included Roger Bannister, Chris Chataway and Norris McWhirter, all athletes whose running skills I admired. It was a place to meet people from other colleges rather than confine yourself to only meeting people from your own college. Jeffrey Archer invited The Beatles and brought them there for dinner, which was a major event at the time. That is what made Oxford so special to me, that it was possible to meet people from different countries, cultures and backgrounds and they were as interested in your world as you were in theirs. The international student life there was exceptional. It was a focal point for students to learn about a whole range of very different lifestyles and beliefs.

I played for Oxford every Wednesday and Friday and was selected for the Varsity Game at Twickenham. At the end of the Easter term I was invited to play with London Welsh in the Middlesex Sevens at Twickenham, something I couldn't turn down. It was a wonderful occasion with a full house and a carnival atmosphere.

* * *

For my father to have a son at Oxford University was beyond his dreams and also outside his comfort zone. Both my parents came to visit me and enjoyed a tour of all the colleges and tea with me in Merton College. My father gazed around the hall in starry-eyed amazement at what was before him. We had tea in the Senior Common Room, reserved for postgraduate students, an oak-panelled room full of beautiful antique furniture. It was an awe-inspiring room, full of history, and to my parents it was like landing on a different planet, far from their small mining village. Cakes and tea were provided on nice china and my parents and I enjoyed the beautiful thirteenth century surroundings and historic architecture. The following morning my father was back down the mine in Tumble Colliery by 6 a.m. My mother's words were very important to me: 'Paid ag anghofio dy hunan' – remember who you are.

My father loved all the new college friends that I brought home – Australians, Americans and Europeans gave him their insights from all over the globe. As he had never even been on a plane himself, their different stories and lifestyles were interesting and exciting to him. My parents were fascinated by their accents and different ways of life and were welcoming to everyone I brought home, and I was proud of them for that.

Lots of good friends came to stay: Rhodes scholars such as Richard Nottage, who became the New Zealand ambassador in Tokyo; Dr Ian McCloskey, director of the Prince of Wales Medical Research Institution in Sydney; J Mark Reifer, personal assistant to Senator Dodds of New Jersey, America, and John Collinge, later the high commissioner to the UK from New Zealand. They loved staying with my mother and father. They enjoyed the local pub in the village and my mother's welsh cakes. They loved coming to the rugby club, enjoyed the beauty of the Gower and Pembrokeshire coastlines and attending the thriving market town of Carmarthen to see the cattle dealing. Local people in Pontyberem arranged with mining officials to take them underground and my friends really appreciated the way the community opened their doors to them. My parents could see that rugby offered me a wonderful future ahead and my family, my sisters Thelma and Yvonne, and brother, Terry, were united in their warm Welsh welcome to players and their families from all rugby nations for many years.

I became a management trainee in Newport and could no longer travel there from Llanelli to train and play each week on top of work. Travelling to Llanelli by car in those days took over two hours. Keith Rowlands, who later became president of the Welsh Rugby Union, had been on the Lions tour in 1962 and he wanted me to come to play for his team, Cardiff. It was time for a change and, once again, my father's response was to give me the space to make the decision for myself. I chose the club in the capital city, enjoyed my time at Cardiff very much and played over a hundred matches for them. Llanelli had been wonderful to me, particularly in nurturing and encouraging me during my formative years. I owed a great deal to the club.

* * *

My last game for Wales was in 1966 against France in the Five Nations Championship at the National Stadium, Cardiff. It was the best way to end – at home with a 9-8 win. Alun Pask was a very talented player and a great captain. He led by example and was a shrewd judge of the game. Our opponents included French greats like the Boniface brothers and Camberabero, but they held no fears for us. This was a French team full of panache, with a flair and confidence in their skills, but we were determined and at home. I had enjoyed many great years in rugby, but I felt I should start concentrating on my career and my future. It was a good game to go out on. No regrets. It was time for me to bow out, having achieved all that I wanted to for my teams and my country.

* * *

There was one more tough rugby experience to come. I was picked for the Lions tour to Australia and New Zealand, very different to the South African one. New Zealand is always a hard tour because of the weather, but it's harder again because of the opponents. For those who say rugby is a religion in Wales, experience New Zealand! I was away from May to September, with six weeks in Australia and three and a half months in New Zealand, and we played two games in Canada on the way home. Rugby is a deep-rooted part of the culture in New Zealand and they recognised just how much the Welsh love their sport too.

It was a disappointing tour. We did well in Australia, winning all our games and two Tests, but we didn't succeed in New Zealand. We left sub-tropical temperatures in Sydney and Brisbane to arrive to a freezing and wet Invercargill day – from the land of pineapples and bananas to the land of ice cold! It was like going back to a severe winter. The All Blacks were outstanding, with Colin (Pinetree) Meads – definitely one of the greatest players ever and named his country's Player of the Century. Herewini, Laidlaw and Lochore were powerful and supreme. The side was extremely – and rightly – confident. The weather and conditions were atrocious and it was hard to keep up spirits. From there we went to Otago and windy Wellington, spending our free time reading and playing cards to stay out of the weather. I was lucky to know people in the country and so was invited to dinner with families I knew, relishing the joy of home cooking and a warm house!

In the first Test at Carisbrook, we lost badly, and again in the second Test in Wellington. Sadly, we lost the third and fourth Tests and we left feeling as miserable as the conditions. To lose the four Tests in New Zealand was hard to bear. Sadly, to travel that far was impossible for my parents. I would have loved them to have shared in what I was able to experience. It was a very different rugby world then. For me, too, it was the end of rugby and the start of a new era in my life.

I arrived home to learn that my mother had been filling the pantry with hams and meats to celebrate my first meal back at home; she was not to know that we had spent the tour being offered steak and eggs for breakfast. For the first week, all of us had gone mad eating everything on offer, but by day five all we wanted was plain cereal. She was desperately disappointed to learn that all I really wanted for my first meal back was a tomato sandwich!

* * *

Rugby has given me so much, on and off the field. Together with my wife Ann, I have made friends from every walk of life, visiting countries my father could only dream of, and learned how to work as a team player and as a leader. It developed my character and it taught me skills for life. I met rugby greats like Bleddyn Williams, Carwyn James, Lewis Jones and Onllwyn Brace who were tremendous, inspirational figures to me. They were very special and would have been great in any rugby era. Later heroes of mine were France's amazing Serge Blanco, the former record-try-scoring Wallaby, David Campese, and the Welsh wizards, Shane Williams and Leigh Halfpenny. Of course, who wouldn't add Sir Gareth Edwards, Gerald Davies and Barry John (The King) to that list?

Rugby union has changed. In my day, it was an amateur game with a different structure and standards. It has been a marvellous tutor and friend throughout my life. Rugby gave me the opportunities of fellowship and camaraderie. I shared happiness and disappointment with teams who played together and for each other. Playing well and giving your best mattered. Conducting yourself properly on and off the field, whether winning or losing, was a given. Even though my father didn't play rugby, he understood all of those qualities learnt also from his 'team' underground. Most of my contemporaries went to work in the mines. Rugby and an education gave me an opportunity and a chance for another life. I have much to be thankful for.

In the professional game, money changes the motivation. Fame is a depreciating asset – what matters is quality of life. You can be cock of the walk one day and the next a feather duster! I hope the present-day players enjoy the game as much as I did, appreciate all that comes their way and make long-lasting friendships. Both of my children, Mark and Sara, are sporty and my grandchildren too and I want them, and future generations, to love and enjoy sport safely.

CHAPTER TWO

Introduction by Delme Thomas
Llanelli RFC, Barbarians, Wales, British and Irish Lions

I was an established Llanelli player in the late sixties when I first came across Derek Quinnell. His reputation as a very talented youth player from Trimsaran had gone before him. He made his senior debut for the Scarlets at the age of eighteen and I quickly realised that this young, but gentle, giant was special. I could see even then that he had the potential to become a great player. He had a quiet confidence about him; nothing would hold him back. He moved seamlessly into the senior squad and was a firm favourite both on and off the field.

Like Derek, I was fortunate enough to play for Llanelli at a young age and had been extremely proud to be selected for the 1966 Lions. As fate would have it, the two of us would become teammates not just for the Scarlets, but in the red Lions jersey on the tour to New Zealand in 1971.

One of his greatest fans in those early days was his girlfriend, now wife, Medora. Coming from a family of great rugby players (including the wonderful Barry John), she knew more about rugby than most men and never missed a game when he was playing.

Derek and I often shared a room at away matches and on tour. As both of us were Welsh speakers, we had a lot in common and enjoyed each other's company. I have to say that he wasn't the tidiest of roommates. He was a lot of fun but always the last to the bus for training, last getting out of the showers and the last going back to the hotel!

His performances for Llanelli certainly caught the eye of the British Lions selectors and he was chosen to be part of the squad to tour New Zealand before winning his first Welsh cap. Here he teamed up again with his Llanelli club coach, Carwyn James, the ultimate motivator, who succeeded in getting the very best out of every individual player. Derek responded brilliantly and gave a hundred per cent in every game. The series in New Zealand was tied at 1-1, so Carwyn, manager Doug Smith and captain John Dawes realised the third Test was absolutely crucial. Derek was brought in to play at blindside wing forward with the sole aim of stopping the danger man, All Black scrum half Sid Going. Derek did a wonderful job that day; we won, and subsequently went on to win the series. Unfortunately, Derek was injured and didn't play in the last Test, which was drawn, but he had done his work and Carwyn's plan had been successful.

A year later, Derek and I played against the All Blacks again, but this time for Llanelli, as coach Carwyn tried to repeat the Lions victory on home soil. I was fortunate enough to be captain that day and we managed to beat Seland Newydd in an historic 9-3 win. Llanelli, in those days, was a busy, working man's town, but it is estimated that on that Tuesday afternoon in October, twenty thousand passionate supporters came to Stradey Park. The town came to a standstill and witnessed a piece of rugby history. Although I didn't remember it at the time, a photograph in the following morning's newspaper showed me being carried off by Derek and another teammate. How he had the strength to do that after such a fierce encounter, I don't know, but it was a lovely gesture, so typical of the man.

There isn't a day goes by that I don't think of that wonderful occasion, and I know all the team – Derek included – said that it was the most magical day of their rugby careers. It was a great victory for Carwyn and for Llanelli.

Derek Quinnell – a great player, a great friend, a great man.

Derek Quinnell

Llanelli RFC, Wales, British and Irish Lions

Although I have been fortunate enough to travel the world as a result of my rugby playing, my roots are firmly in Carmarthenshire, West Wales.

I was brought up just outside Llanelli in a little village called Trimsaran, and in that village there were always kids available to play with after school or in the schoolyard. We didn't have a rugby pitch in those days, so I played soccer, which I thoroughly enjoyed, although the schoolyard was pretty unforgiving. I went to Trimsaran Junior School where any kind of a game involving a ball would do: cricket, soccer, tennis or rugby – I loved them all! I then attended Coleshill Secondary Modern School, which is probably where I first started to play team rugby.

There were hardly any cars in those days. I remember the first car coming to our street and it parked right in the middle of the road, which was actually, at any given time, our football or cricket pitch or tennis court. We asked the owner to move the car to the end of the road so we could reclaim our 'sporting facility' and, fair play, he did!

Day, or night under streetlights, we dreamt of playing in big stadiums, but the street had to do.

Playing a game was all that mattered and everybody took part. One thing that always sticks out in my mind was the summer holidays. The soccer matches we played started early, usually around ten o'clock in the morning. For a couple of hours maybe it would only be three- or four-a-side then, as the day wore on, players were interchangeable as children came and went, for shopping expeditions with their mams, family calls or just for food! It was fabulous. People just turned up and asked, 'Who am I playing for?' and you'd say to them, 'You're on that team' or 'this team'. As a result, you could hardly move on the field due to the number of players, so close quarter skills were encouraged as the day wore on. Very often, some of the boys who had already played earlier in the day came back to join the match, and those who had just finished work gulped their tea down quickly so they could go and play soccer. So about twelve hours after the original kick-off, hordes of young people of all ages would have joined in and the score (as if anybody was counting) was at least two hundred goals to ninety-nine! We went home in the dark, tired but very happy.

At Coleshill Secondary Modern School, games were

far more structured and organised. Concrete, and our village ground, gave way to proper pitches. Mervyn Bowen, a former Scarlets full back, was our PE master and he was terrific. We learnt so much about all sports from him, but I soon chose rugby. It was a game I was comfortable with and I enjoyed playing. I was in the same form as Phil Bennett and, from that early age, you could see that he was something very special. The rest of us were in a different league and just made up the numbers.

I played for the school and then for Llanelli and District schoolboys. We got to the final of the Dewar Shield, the big competition for under-15s and eventually lost to Bridgend. Later, Coleshill Secondary Modern actually won the famous Llanelli Schoolboys Sevens, which was normally won by the local grammar school. This was quite an achievement, as the tournament attracted all the best schoolboy teams like Millfield. Our team was composed of Phil Bennett and six others, and the taste of victory added enormously to my enjoyment of the game. That, and the will to win, is pretty important in the psychology of playing rugby football.

* * *

My family background was sporting, but not in rugby. My dad, who came from Sussex originally, was a former marine commando. He did a bit of boxing and played soccer, too, in his youth. My uncle was an army boxing champion and he played soccer until he was fifty years of age.

Since then, starting with me, it has been rugby football, which has played an important part in our family life. I left school at fifteen and joined the Llanelli Youth side; I never actually had a junior club. I played four years for the youth team and then, at the age of eighteen, I started playing for the Scarlets, my one and only club.

My heroes at school were the senior boys who played rugby. I looked up to them and thought they were special and wanted to be like them. Playing for the youth side in Llanelli, little did I think that later I would be rubbing shoulders with the likes of Delme Thomas. I remember seeing him in the car park, coming back from the 1966 Lions tour, looking so smart in his Lions blazer. I marvelled at what a local boy had achieved. I thought, 'How fantastic is that?' Five years later, I was with him on the next Lions tour to New Zealand. It couldn't have turned out better.

After good performances for Llanelli, I'd been on the bench for Wales for a little while from 1970, but never gained that elusive first cap. In 1971, I was working as an electrician. I'd served my five-year apprenticeship, as you had to in those days, and then, when I finished that, went to work on the first one-pound-an-hour jobs at Baglan Bay. We were a crew of sparks, welders and engineers building a new BP plant.

DEREK QUINNELL

I had only been there four months when I was selected to go on the Lions tour. We knew the side was being announced on the Tuesday lunchtime so we all gathered in the cabin where we had our lunch, listening to the news on the radio. They announced the squad, position by position, so, being a back row player, I was one of the last names to be announced. There were murmurings after each name, but others were shushing and saying 'Quiet!' so that we could hear the entire squad. When my name was read out, pandemonium broke out! In fairness, all the guys were terrific and we all finished early that day and went for a celebratory pint or two in the Ferry Boat Inn in Briton Ferry. The lads were very supportive and so was the company I worked for, even though I wouldn't be there to finish the job. They actually made me redundant, which gave me an extra week's pay. This was fantastic, because the out of pocket allowance on a Lions tour was ten shillings a day – three pounds fifty a week – so on a tour lasting four months I would earn the princely sum of about fifty pounds, hardly a fortune, but what I was about to experience was priceless.

The build-up for what turned out to be an historic tour was nothing like the preparations for today's British and Irish Lions. We gathered for a short time in Eastbourne and were put through our paces by coach Carwyn James and tour manager Doug Smith. Today, the kit alone fills several articulated lorries. In those days, it was totally different. We had to take our own white shirts and grey slacks, but were given one jumper. In addition, we were given two blazers, one of which was a dress blazer with a little badge on, with a dicky bow for formal dinners, and the other a big-badged version which you wore to most events. We had two jerseys and two sets of kit, which were supposed to last for the whole tour. The reality was that, having been rucked several times by the New Zealanders, a number of the jerseys had big rips in them and had to be sewn up! At the end of the tour, we were allowed to retain one jersey and were expected to swap the other with an All Black. The shrunken shirts were in a sorry state but I still treasure that first Lions jersey.

The Lions tour to New Zealand in 1971 was tough as we had a squad of thirty players to play twenty-six matches. Nowadays, they go on tour with a much larger squad to play far fewer matches. In those days, also, anyone getting injured would have to go home and a replacement would be flown in, as we were only allowed thirty players on tour at any given time. I think this brought us a lot closer together, as everyone had a part to play. There were times when, if somebody in your position was injured, you would have to play on the Saturday, the Wednesday, and then the following Saturday. You were either injured and had to go home, or injured and able to recover in a reasonably short space of time. Amazingly, we toured without a physiotherapist or a team doctor!

What we actually had was a manager, and an assistant manager who was also the coach. We picked up a physiotherapist in New Zealand and, fortunately, Doug Smith, our manager, was a doctor, so he was able to hold his own little surgeries on a Sunday or Monday morning and diagnose any medical problems, which could be put right using the facilities of the local hospitals. A Lions tour leaving now would have its own management team, coaches, statisticians, a doctor and two or three physios who would work with the side. The back-up team in New Zealand in 2005 was seventeen strong, whereas we had a skeleton staff. The togetherness that we had when the thirty-two people got on that plane to play twenty-six matches thousands of miles away from home was quite remarkable.

For a twenty-one-year-old to be touring in New Zealand and playing against people they had only read about was fantastic! It was a great learning curve in so many respects, and actually to win a series 'down under' was remarkable, the first, and as yet only, time that the Lions won a Test series against the All Blacks. I was there at the right time, in the company of an exceptional group of players. We were a tight-knit unit who worked hard, on and off the field.

The tour didn't get off to the most promising of starts, as we lost the first game in Australia.

Amazingly, we arrived in Brisbane on a Monday afternoon and the following Wednesday played against Queensland. Nowadays, they talk about jet lag, advising that you shouldn't do anything for forty-eight hours after flying, but the next thing we knew we were playing the first match of the tour. They came at us like a bunch of banshees and, in fairness, played quite well. I think we lost by a couple of points. During the game, I was running across the field and Irish flanker Fergus Slattery ran past me saying 'Come on Quinners! Come on Quinners!' and I thought 'Hell! What's going on?' Five minutes later, I was running past Slats saying 'Come on Slats, come on Slats,' but our legs had gone – we were on a different planet!

That first week or so was very tough, and, although we had spent a short time together in Eastbourne doing, as someone said, high altitude training, we were shattered. Losing that first game was probably a good wake up call for us. When we came off the field, we thought, 'What's happened here?' That brought us together very quickly.

We won the second game in New South Wales on the Saturday, then travelled to New Zealand. I played the first game there and we won quite comfortably, but suddenly came the realisation we were now into the hard part of the tour. That first defeat taught us a valuable lesson as well: no matter how good you are – or how good you *think* you are – if the tour itinerary isn't right and is too onerous, and ours certainly was, then you are under pressure right from the start. Looking back, I often think why the hell did they organise that first game less than forty-eight hours after arriving in Australia? How '*twp*' was that? But it did put us in good stead really.

The management had to take a great deal of credit for the team ethos. Doug Smith was a former Lion and Carwyn James a former international. Carwyn was way ahead of his time with his philosophy, both in the way that he thought about the game and the way he got the best out of the players. We, in turn, responded well, and that first game in Australia and the second Test against the All Blacks were the only games we lost; this was unheard of before or since.

What made this tour very special was that everyone bought into the team ethic and played their hearts out in every game. Just as important to a successful tour are the players who don't make the Test team but contribute so much by winning the mid-week matches. This adds to the momentum of the tour.

I think that its success was due to a number of contributory factors. We had a squad of extremely talented players, several of whom were world-class. Carwyn James, as the coach, was an excellent man-manager and knew precisely what to do in order to get the best out of each player. He also recognised the talent within the opposition. He was able to pinpoint any strengths and weaknesses and replicate those in training and focus on what was needed to do to beat them. 'Stopping at source' was a favourite line of his. He had identified Sid Going, the All Black's wonderful scrum half, as a real danger man and I was drafted into the third Test team as a blindside wing forward to 'Stop Sid'. On the training field, in the week prior to that Test match, one of our scrum halves, Chico Hopkins, had to play the role of Sid Going and became thoroughly fed up of me tackling him at every opportunity!

As well as playing ability, our happy band of tourists also possessed great durability and, out of the thirty players originally selected, only three had to be replaced. Incredibly, all three, Mick Hipwell, Sandy Carmichael and Ray McLoughlin, were injured in the one game against Canterbury, just a week before the first Test, but this huge setback only served to create an even tighter unit of players.

Finally, I think that the weather also played a part in our victorious tour. We possessed a creative, speedy and talented set of backs, which Carwyn wanted to exploit at every opportunity, but slick handling and passing is always easier with a dry ball! Out of the twenty-four matches played in New Zealand, only two were staged in wet conditions, which suited us down to the ground. It was no wonder therefore that our tour party wingers, Gerald Davies, David Duckham, John

Bevan and Alistair Biggar, saw so much of the ball. To be fair, the New Zealand public, although hurt by the defeats that we inflicted on their teams, appreciated and applauded our style of rugby.

* * *

The other Lions tours I went on, to New Zealand in 1977 and South Africa in 1980, never quite lived up to that wonderful experience I had as a twenty-one-year-old in 1971. Down under the second time, the weather was appalling for most of the matches and for our training sessions. It was the tour of the 'soggy wet kit' and we were forever trying to dry our clothes on hotel radiators. Willie Duggan, the Blackrock College and Irish international, overcame this problem with a novel idea of his own. Having sent home his official tracksuit and wet suit, he proceeded to train in a white T-shirt, shorts and grey socks. He used the same kit every day! The shorts became manky and the T-shirt a horrible grey colour, until by the end none of us, his teammates, would go anywhere near him. He just occupied a solitary corner in any dressing room. He didn't bother with laundry, had very little kit to carry around and, secretly, we quite admired his minimalist approach to touring!

In many ways, we could have won, or at least drawn, the 1977 series. Unusually, we had parity in the forwards, but the All Blacks never know when they are beaten. In the final Test, it all came down to the last minute, when they scored in the corner to clinch the series 3-1. At least I still had '71 to look back on!

1980 in South Africa was also a case of what might have been. The team was captained very well by William Blackledge (Billy) Beaumont, now Chairman of World Rugby, and managed and coached by the two former Irish internationals, Syd Millar and Noel Murphy. By now, Lions tours had a team doctor, in this case, the redoubtable Dr Jack Matthews who had, in the company of Bleddyn Williams, formed a most potent centre partnership for Wales in the late 1940s and early 1950s. Dr Jack was a hard man and, in an amateur boxing bout in South Wales in the forties, held Rocky Marciano to a draw, something no professional opponent could ever achieve, as Marciano retired as undefeated World Heavyweight Champion.

Although we won all the provincial matches, we lost the series 3-1. I am convinced that the main reason for this was that we weren't able to field the same pair of half backs in any of the four Test matches. Injuries to players such as Terry Holmes and Gareth Davies were to prove costly, as was losing English props, Phil Blakeway and Fran Cotton, but you can't legislate for such events. The Fran Cotton episode was one of the scariest things on tour. He collapsed on the field and said to me, 'Quinners, I think I'm having a heart attack.' He was stretchered off by four young boys who could barely lift him, begging them, 'Please don't drop me.' Fran was examined by the pioneering, world-renowned heart transplant surgeon Christiaan Barnard who, after completing his investigation said, 'There is good news and bad news. The good news is that it's not your heart and, even if it was, I could give you a new one. The bad news is that you've had a kind of virus which means that you won't play again for two to three months.' Incidents like that put things into sharp perspective.

* * *

If 1971 and the Lions tour to New Zealand was memorable, so too was the following year. In March, I finally got to play for Wales and in October I was part of another historic victory as my beloved Llanelli beat the All Blacks 9-3. This was the day that all rugby followers claimed, 'I was there!' And this was the day all the pubs in Llanelli ran dry. What Carwyn had done as coach to the Lions, he now repeated in his own back yard and plotted a remarkable victory that is now part of rugby folklore. As Max Boyce sang:

'Now all the little babies in Llanelli from now on will be christened Roy or Carwyn, Derek, Delme, Phil or John.
And in a hundred years from now, they'll sing a song for me
'bout the day the scoreboard read Llanelli 9, Seland Newydd 3.'

RUGBY GENERATIONS

When I came on the field as a substitute in that first game for Wales in 1972, against France, is one of the most repeated clips on screen and yet I was only on the field for about two minutes. I remember I was sitting up in the stand and, in those days, those of us on the bench had to take it in turns to be in charge of the sweets, which meant you had to go out and buy them!

Normally they were market (pick and mix) sweets – a mixture that you just sucked so that you didn't have a dry mouth. At that time, you were told not to drink water or you'd have colic. It was nonsense, because nowadays the medics say take plenty of water on board to make sure you're hydrated. All of a sudden in the match, Mervyn Davies, 'Swerve', went down. You weren't allowed to warm up or do anything like that then. I had to run all the way down the steps and get to the medical room, where the doctor had to declare the injured player was unfit to continue before you could go on as a replacement. You couldn't just swap over like today and take one player off and put another player on. Clive Rowlands, our coach, was with Swerve and the doctor pleading, 'Can he go on? Can he go on?' and the doctor said firmly, 'Please … wait a minute, I'm examining.' It was all very formal. We were down to fourteen men all this time and eventually the doctor said, 'OK. Go on.' Clive ushered me out and, by this time, everybody was gathering at the entrance of the ground in the tunnel. There were also policemen everywhere waiting to escort people off the field at the end of the game. As I rushed to get on the field, I barged a policeman and knocked his helmet off. I bought him beer for twenty years to make up for this until he left the force!

Finally, I got on the pitch and I realised I was still eating the boiled sweet, so I hurriedly spat it out. In the two minutes that was left in the game, I ran about like a headless chicken, desperate to follow the ball. When the final whistle went, I was absolutely knackered. I'd only been on the field a very short time, but I was totally drained. I had lunch the day after at my parents' house and, when I walked in, the first thing my mam said to me was not congratulations but, 'I don't know, the first thing you did when you ran on to the pitch was to spit! *Ych a fi.* Fancy spitting!' She didn't realise it was a sweet I was getting rid of, and still gave me a good row for spitting.

I gained twenty-three caps playing for Wales over the course of ten years. I also played against countries like Fiji, Argentina and Romania where caps weren't awarded. They weren't given to substitutes either and I sat on the bench for another twenty-five games for Wales.

Every aspect of the game now is so different from when I played. My era was more physical – dirty even – because then there weren't all the television cameras, the replays and the citings, which are so much part of the game now. Today's players, even the backs, have muscles on muscles because of strict conditioning, diet and training regimes. Are they as durable? I'm not so sure. There are more one-to-one physical confrontations these days and I sometimes yearn for a more skills-based game.

* * *

Playing for Wales and playing for the Lions was something very special. For Wales, I was fortunate that of the twenty-three matches I played in, I lost only four and two of them were against New Zealand. I never lost against England, although I faced them on five occasions. The Welsh team I was part of won four Triple Crowns on the trot and two Grand Slams – quite a record!

Those Welsh teams, like the Lions teams I played in, were full of extremely gifted players and I consider myself very fortunate to have worn the same red jerseys as them. Every time you mention the seventies in rugby circles, people immediately, and quite rightly, talk of Barry, Gareth, Phil, Gerald, JJ and JPR – first names or initials that conjure up moments of rugby magic.

As a mere forward, I look back at players like Fran Cotton and Peter Wheeler of England, the Irish quartet Fergus Slattery, Willie John McBride, Willie Duggan and Moss Keane. I remember too Scotland's Mighty

Mouse and our own Welsh 'Pontypool Front Row', Charlie, Bobby and Graham. These were all great players, all great characters. They played their hearts out, but managed to enjoy the social side as well.

As a back row player, I have to say that the best I've ever played with or seen was 'Merv the Swerve', Mervyn Davies. The lanky, six-foot-six number eight played on two Lions tours and was made captain of Wales in 1975. It is a tragedy that a brain haemorrhage cut short his fantastic playing career. He dominated the lineout, tackled everything that moved, and fell on the ball with little concern for his own safety as marauding forwards kicked lumps out of him.

The friendships made within teams at home and on tour can last a lifetime and create a bond that can never be broken. In 2013, I was invited, along with other members of the '71 Lions, to attend a dinner in Dublin organised by Terenure College. The College had been attended by Mick Hipwell, one of the three players injured in that infamous Lions v Canterbury game. The organisers were anxious to raise funds for its rugby teams and came up with the idea of honouring one of their former students, Mick Hipwell, Terenure's first Irish international player. Twenty-five out of the thirty-three Lions turned up that evening, the absentees being either unwell or having sadly passed away. Six hundred guests assembled that night in Dublin, a lot of money was raised for the college but, more importantly, a group of rugby players were able to meet again, share reminiscences and renew friendships.

The last international game I played was, fittingly, against New Zealand in 1980. For me, they were the bar to measure all others against. I had no regrets – other than the fact we didn't win! I realised that it was time for me to retire from international rugby. I'd thoroughly enjoyed my sporting career and I had achieved all that I could. The game wasn't professional then and I had to consider the future for my family and myself. I wanted it to be my decision and I knew the time was right. My mam had been going on at me for years telling me I should give up this 'silly game' as I was a family man now, but ultimately it had to be my decision alone. It was still a sad time to have to stop, though I played two more years with Llanelli, which I enjoyed. Of course, I missed the cut and thrust of international rugby, but it was a relief not to have to go training at places like the Afan Lido, but just to have a couple of beers and go home.

Llanelli is the only club I've ever played for and it's very important to me. In 1986 I bought a house looking down on Stradey Park, looking forward to a time when I would be older, but would be able to walk down, have a couple of beers, watch a game and walk back home. Then they moved the ground three miles down the road! When I did eventually retire, I trained with the youth team and eventually coached them for a number of years. I then coached the national side with Tony Gray for three years.

The new purpose-built stadium, Parc y Scarlets, is superb, but Stradey Park will always be a special place as it has been so much a part of my life. There is so much history attached to it. There was a legacy there, with old traditions and wonderful memories. You could smell the liniment in the dressing rooms, and imagine the characters who had pulled on the red jersey there over the years. The thing about going to Stradey Park was that you knew where everybody would be – the guys from Carmarthen would meet up and have a couple of pints and, in those days, we used to go into the bar after the game. We'd have our food upstairs and mix with the vice presidents and then go down to the bar and mix with the supporters. The same characters would stay and hang about, enjoying such a special place with special people.

I couldn't have enjoyed the playing or working career I've had without the love and support of my family. My parents were always behind me and kept my feet firmly on the ground. They never said a great deal, but were just there in the background, there when I needed them and, secretly, I think were quite proud of all that I achieved.

My wife, Medora, tells me that she knows more about rugby than I do. She doesn't, but she has been the most wonderful wife and mother, who has fed and looked after four big, strapping men. Our three sons have enjoyed rugby success in their own right. Craig won thirty-two Welsh caps and Scott over fifty caps in Union and League, as well as playing in three Tests for the Lions. Unfortunately, our youngest son, Gavin, lost an eye playing rugby, a stark reminder of how perilous this great game can be.

I never forced the boys to play, they found their own way much as I did. Craig was once asked was it hard for him growing up with a famous rugby-playing dad and he said, 'No, he's just Dad. Just my dad,' which I thought was lovely. Naturally, I worried when I watched the boys play, it's a tough old sport and some of the confrontations between Craig and Scott when they opposed one another could be quite fierce. The Welsh World Cup final referee, Nigel Owens, once warned the two of them of dire consequences during a particularly heated exchange. He said, 'If you don't stop now, I'll tell your mother!' They stopped immediately ... In fact, all the Quinnells, father and sons, have stopped playing nowadays and both Medora and I are quite glad about that.

CHAPTER THREE

Introduction by Rhys Williams
Cardiff Blues, Barbarians, Wales

Every Welsh rugby fan remembers 1999 and *that* try scored by Scott Gibbs at Wembley to deny England the Grand Slam. There was another iconic moment for me in that game, the wonderful sight of Craig Quinnell, ball in hand, steam-rollering Steve Hanley, the six-foot-four Sale winger. Hanley, who had just scored a try for England, I'm sure couldn't have believed how his fortunes could change so quickly, but as anyone who has met, or played with or against, Craig will testify that his barnstorming run was par for the course. CQ, as he is affectionately known, is larger than life – a force of nature. I count myself very fortunate to have played with two of the three brothers, Scott and Craig. How wonderful would it have been for Wales if younger brother Gavin could have joined them in the same international team!

RUGBY GENERATIONS

When I first played for Cardiff RFC, it was quite something for me as a newcomer to see players of the calibre of Rob Howley, Dai Young, Jonathan Humphreys and Neil Jenkins arrive for training sessions. One day, as I turned up in my B reg Talbot Horizon, I witnessed a most extraordinary sight: a BMW sports car arrived noisily and out popped this towering figure. It was as if the car had given birth, and the new arrival there in the car park was Craig Quinnell. He enjoyed nice cars and the finer things of life, but was the most welcoming of characters and a great mentor to the young players like myself who were coming through the ranks. He was a great friend, a huge presence in every sense, happy to chat and the type of player and teammate who would always light up and enliven any room he entered.

I learnt quite quickly some very important things about CQ. In training, do not run into him when he's holding the pad, because Newton's law of equal and opposite reaction is true – trust me! Although he is not a big drinker, do not take him on when he's had a couple. You get to know very quickly that the effect a pint has on a five-foot-ten-and-a-half, thirteen stone three quarter isn't quite the same as on a second row forward of Craig's stature. Lastly, do not volunteer to spot for him in the gym. You could do yourself some serious damage just by lifting one of his training weights!

INTRODUCTION: RHYS WILLIAMS

I feel honoured to have played with the big guy. I always enjoy the times we meet up, a feeling that I know is echoed by his teammates and supporters alike. Cardiff fans have always appreciated good and aggressive forward play, so it is little wonder that Craig was such an Arms Park favourite with his bullocking runs, forearm smashes and the occasional heavyweight boxing match.

I'll always remember playing against Gloucester at Kingsholm in the quarter final of the Heineken Cup in 2001. The Cherry and White supporters, particularly those in the infamous 'shed', are a feisty and passionate crowd. You could sense just before kick-off that, as the visiting team, we were in for a tough time. CQ was unfazed and took great delight in running up and down the touchline in front of the 'shed', tormenting the Gloucester supporters and revelling in the role of the big, bad guy. It incensed them, but delighted our large band of travelling fans!

Craig is a very special, larger than life character. He has a heart of gold and always makes time for teammates, his fans and the many charities he supports. Even when he was yellow carded, he got a big cheer from the crowd. Always in the thick of things, you could never ignore CQ. He is a great ambassador for the game and a wonderful member of the extraordinary Quinnell rugby dynasty ... what else would you expect?

Craig Quinnell

Llanelli RFC, Richmond, Cardiff RFC, Cardiff
Blues, Saracens, Worcester, Barbarians, Wales

I always played sport at school – rugby, soccer, cricket, tennis and squash. You name it; I've tried it! In athletics, I gave everything a go, the field events shot put and discus, and I even graced the track, running in the 100m race on sports day! Sport was so much a part of my life in every way growing up.

From a young age, I remember whenever we went anywhere with Dad, there was always someone who wanted to talk to him, ask for his autograph, or have a picture with him. It was normal for us three boys, his sons, and we were used to it. People wanted to shake his hand or tell him their memories of his games. We didn't know why and we didn't care, because to us he was just Dad. Everyone knew him locally and my uncle Barry (John) was just as important it seemed! I can remember going to a charity football match that they were both playing in and being amazed at the crowds who turned up to see them. They were like the Royal Family, waving and smiling. I was far more impressed to find out that the tallest man in the UK was playing as well and I wanted to see *him*!

As a youngster, I never felt any pressure because my dad was famous. Any pressure, if there ever was any, came from following my brother Scott. That competiveness was good for me, though, as it kept me on my toes. Just like any younger sibling following an older brother through school, there were always comparisons made. Five Roads Junior was a very small school of about seventy pupils in total. Everyone knew one another in our very close-knit community. Scott was always the good kid and I was the naughty one, and people were fond of telling me, 'You need to be more like your brother!' At the time, I was in the top set in school for my subjects and I couldn't understand why they wanted me to be more like him.

Scott and I played in the same school team, even though he was ten or eleven and I was eight years old, and it was always good to have my big brother on my side. It was much better than playing against him! I then went on to play for Llanelli under-11s and played for the school and district teams when I moved up to Graig Comprehensive. Once again, in that school, Scott got on well with the games teachers, while I had the reputation for being the unruly one. I was regularly blamed for any misdemeanours and I suppose I responded to that. I don't think I was aware at the time of how good it was to be one of the first to be picked for any school team. I only wanted to go out there and do my best and play sport, whatever sport it was!

At the age of sixteen I gained a scholarship to Llandovery College in Carmarthenshire, a school with a proud rugby history. The Carwyn James Scholarship was a very important one to us. He was a very close friend and mentor to my dad and his links to Llanelli made the honour all the greater. I actually had the room where he used to live in the college, and that was very important to me, because Carwyn James was one of the most influential coaches in world rugby.

I played for Llandovery College and Carmarthenshire, Wales Schools, then Wales Youth and under-21s. My claim to fame is that I played for Wales at the age of twenty, the youngest of us all to represent our country at international level. That was a very proud achievement for me in a family such as ours. Dad counters that by saying that he did all of those things, but couldn't have played for Welsh schools as he left at the age of fifteen and so wasn't eligible!

After gaining my A levels in PE and Business Studies, I went to Loughborough University to study Sports Science. It didn't last long though – one term! University wasn't for me. I didn't enjoy playing rugby there, and was the only freshman in the first fifteen. It didn't feel like being part of a proper team to me.

I came home, but straight away Dad informed me, in no uncertain terms, 'You're not working for me!' I went instead to train with Llanelli and started playing with them, but after two weeks of just enjoying myself, Dad intervened again with, 'Get to work!'

One of the conditions for employing me at his company, Aquatreat, was that I had to go back to college and study for a HNC in Chemistry. I found myself a course at Neath Technical College and Swansea University. Dad put his foot down and he was right to do so.

I did the course, as well as working full-time with Dad, and playing for Llanelli. Looking back, it was hard work, but I loved every second of it. Student life wasn't really for me, but working and playing for my home town was exactly what I wanted. My dream as a youngster had always been to play for the Scarlets; they are my team, as they were my dad's and big brother's before me and from a very young age, I'd gone to watch them train. They were the 'big team', the team I most aspired to play for. I began training with the first team from the age of sixteen, so in my heart there was nothing better. My father was on the committee there and also coaching Llanelli Youth; I couldn't have asked for a better home town introduction.

CRAIG QUINNELL

I was training with Peter Herbert, the fitness coach who was a leading developer of the science of sports fitness. He was brilliant and I learnt a great deal from him. A few years later, when I was part of the Wales international squad, he was the fitness coach there. We would discuss training in depth and I enjoyed questioning him about new techniques in training and the reasons we were training in a particular way. He told me, when I was eighteen, that I should go to America to play American football. At that time, I was big, but also quick, so NFL might have been the perfect sport for me as it would have utilised my size. In rugby at the time, all of my training was to be lighter. In contrast today, rugby players are getting bigger and heavier and training is designed for more physical contact. I was constantly told I had to get my weight down and that wasn't good.

We had to be weighed twice a day, which now would be considered pointless but also alarming in terms of body awareness. I would be weighed in the morning before training and then again after training to measure weight loss and dehydration. I used to lie about my weight all of the time. I would say I weighed 130 kg when I actually weighed 135 to 140 kg. I never actually felt any great external pressure to live up to my family's high rugby playing achievements, but the internal pressure was always there. I just wanted to be the best I could be.

Dad was always there for us all. He wasn't a pushy parent, but if you wanted him, he was always there to go and ask for help or advice. Unlike Scott, who he coached in the Llanelli Youth side, he never coached any of the teams I was involved in. As I went away to school, it was different for me. Over the years, he never made comment on things that happened with the professional teams I was involved with. He just used to shake his head knowingly, as if to say, 'Why did you do that?', especially after the sixteen-week ban I got for one of my over-exuberant actions! A newspaper report described me as, 'somewhat undisciplined'. I saw myself as the rugby equivalent of a pantomime villain. My size means people often judge me and are nervous around me, without really knowing me.

I had the opposite of that experience in Disneyland recently when I was with my friends and godchildren. They were all enjoying themselves on a spectacular ride. I was too big for the ride and my godson was too small, so we just went and did our own thing while the others queued for two hours. People came up to me to ask for my autograph and whether they could have selfies with me. My godson kept saying, 'Come on! Why are these people bothering you? I just want to get on with buying a Harry Potter wand.' Having a well-known godfather was strange for him, but I remembered when I was younger, seeing the same thing happening to my dad and my uncle, so I understood what my godson was feeling.

I made my debut for Wales at the age of twenty against Fiji in 1995. Receiving my first cap was a dream come true. I was presented with it by Sir Tasker Watkins VC, then president of the WRU. Sir Tasker, who was small in stature but a legal giant, had shown incredible bravery on the field of battle in World War Two to win his Victoria Cross. It is very fitting that a statue of him welcomes spectators at one of the main entrances of the Principality Stadium in Cardiff.

I can't remember how I heard that I'd been chosen to play, as everything was such a haze of excitement. I really can't remember whether Kevin Bowring, the coach, told me, or whether I heard it on the news. All that mattered to me was that I was selected to play! I do remember rushing to phone Scott who was playing for Wigan rugby league team at the time, to tell him the good news. When the big day came, he travelled down with two mates, Barry McDermott and Terry O'Connor, both Great Britain rugby league internationals. I appreciated very much that they all came down just to watch my first game and to support me. It was just terrific! Going away to stay in a hotel for a few days before the game was absolutely huge to me then. Driving to Cardiff for the first time for a training session was a huge adventure; the rugby itself was far less overwhelming!

We stayed in the Copthorne Hotel in Cardiff before

the Fiji game and I remember one of the props at the time, Lyndon Mustoe, had hidden in the wardrobe, and when I came into the room, he jumped onto me like Cato in the Pink Panther films and I smashed him to the floor! He thought he was sharing a room with Simon Hill and wanted to scare him. He'd actually spent three hours waiting to jump out on Simon and I think he had quite a shock when his roommate turned out to be me!

Looking back, I was just a kid in a man's world – I was nervous and apprehensive about sharing a room with someone I didn't know, but I went on to be great friends and teammates with Lyndon at Cardiff and it's funny how things go full circle; being roommates early on in one's career can lead to lifelong friendships.

The same was true of playing for Llanelli, sitting in the dressing room surrounded by Phil Davies, Andrew Lamerton, Ricky Evans, Tony Copsey and Mark Perego. All these guys had been there, done that and worn the jersey for Llanelli and Wales; to say anything would have been ridiculous. I just listened, trained with them and learnt from them. I used to exercise two or three times a week with Phil Davies and wouldn't have dreamt of questioning a word he said. I sat and listened and then tried to prove myself on the pitch.

That first game against Fiji was a bit of a blur. I remember Kevin Bowring saying before the game, 'Don't worry about carrying the ball, it will all fall into place.' I was told to run off centre, Nigel Davies. Those were my instructions. Unfortunately, Nigel went off injured early in the game and I didn't touch the ball the whole game afterwards. I just hit all the rucks and mauls as effectively as I could, which was the other thing I was told to do. Looking back, it was a poor performance; I didn't get to touch the ball, or play a major role. I wasn't really used to the best of my ability that day, but we somehow managed to win narrowly by 19-15. Luckily, I came back and played other times and showed what I had to offer.

My club career has been quite varied, taking me to teams in England as well as two spells with Cardiff RFC and the newly formed Cardiff Blues when the game went professional. After Llanelli, in 1996, I moved to Richmond to play at my brother Scott's recommendation, and stayed three years. It was a very ambitious club and although only in the second division, had great plans for development and future success. They made a number of big signings including my brother Scott from Wigan and a strong Welsh contingent of players such as Allan Bateman, John Davies and Andy Moore. The club's other name became Richmond Welsh! I had a really great time there; I liked the people, the club and the style of rugby that was being played – we were a family, not just a rugby club.

John Kingston was the coach and I think he was one

of the very best I've worked with. He was way ahead of his time in his use of video analysis; he even managed on occasions to work out the opposition's lineout plays. He created the team and did a brilliant job of moulding amateurs into professionals. Some of the players were in their thirties, brokers in the city who had a very different perspective on life – I'd never met anyone like that before. They had to adapt quickly to the new professional era and it worked.

The team was successful because we'd all been hand-picked. Richmond needed – and the 'amateurs' needed – a few battle-hardened players like myself. Me, I was just looking after my teammates, a bit undisciplined but streetwise, and fully committed to the cause. It really was ground-breaking to bring together a team like this. We still have regular reunions because we got on so well. Many of us had to move and live in London to be part of that team which was a very new experience. We played together on and off the field and still cherish our friendships.

In 1999, I started my first spell with Cardiff RFC. I'd been given a Cardiff shirt when I was young and had always liked the club in the capital city. My uncle Barry had played with great distinction for them, so when I signed I felt great pleasure in being associated with a big club with such a great rugby history. I enjoyed my time there, but I left, after just a few years, feeling that I wasn't really being valued.

There followed two comparatively short stays, one with Saracens and one on a temporary loan to Worcester, where my appetite for the game returned. I'm very thankful to Worcester for giving me the opportunity for that to happen. Then in 2003, I got a call from Dai Young, now the very successful coach of Wasps, but then coach of the newly established Cardiff Blues rugby region. Dai was a friend, so it could potentially have been a difficult situation, but we both understood our respective roles and I became a first team regular in the three seasons I spent there. It was a proud moment for me that a former teammate would want me back. In total, I played over fifty games for the Cardiff club and I enjoyed my time there immensely.

Looking back at my international career, one of the great highlights was in 1999, in the Five Nations Championships, despite a bad start – we had lost the first two games against Scotland (the eventual champions) and Ireland. Although I had missed the Scottish match, I came back from injury to face the boys in green. It was a game we lost narrowly. Personally, it contained highs and lows; I scored a try, but then was sent to the sin bin – the first sin bin in international rugby. Allegedly, I'd hit Keith Wood, the Irish hooker, but I have always blamed Dai Young for starting it!

We then had to travel to Paris to the new Stade de

France to play in front of what was a record crowd of over seventy-eight thousand. We hadn't won on French soil since Mervyn Davies had led Wales to victory in 1975, so to score the winning try in a hard-fought, one point, 33-34 victory was very, very special. I remember Scott and I on the pitch after the game phoning our parents who were staying with Tony Gray, the former Wales coach, and his wife, Mair, in North Wales. 'We've done it, Dad! We've won out here!' we shouted down the phone. 'It's something you never achieved!' It's not many times we were able to say that!

A couple of weeks later, we played against England in what was to be the last Five Nations Championship, as Italy joined the following year. It was a remarkable match in a packed Wembley Stadium, as the new Millennium Stadium was being built. Scott and I were both in the team and the crowd was entertained before kick-off by both Max Boyce and Tom Jones – remember this was a 'home' match. Although we looked to be losing the game, a sensational try in extra time by Scott Gibbs, converted by Neil Jenkins, meant we had won the match and enabled Scotland to pip England for the Championship.

The other highlights for me have been games where I played against and with my two brothers. People could not believe the ferocity of some of the exchanges between Scott and me in club matches between

CRAIG QUINNELL

Llanelli and Cardiff. In the first game we played against each other we kicked off, they knocked on, we had a scrum and Emyr Lewis picked up the ball. Scott tackled him so I jumped on Scott and stood on him with all my weight. In the second half I ran at him and there was a huge collision and the whole crowd went 'Oooo'. We were both flat out on the turf so I stuck my tongue out at Scott and he sucked on it! Brothers eh? After the game he showed me six bruises where my studs had been. There was never any quarter asked or given. We had been hitting and tackling one another since we were kids playing American football in the front passage at home. It was quite natural to take that aggression on to the playing field, although my mother couldn't bear to see us knock lumps out of one another.

I've already mentioned some of the internationals I played in with Scott, but a particular match where I was in the same team as Gavin will stay with me for ever. I had never played rugby with my younger brother before, but we were both selected to play for the Barbarians in the Mobbs memorial match against East Midlands at Bedford, in March 2006. Between us we scored seven tries, six to me and one for my little brother. The crowd were booing me in the end every time I scored. I'm not sure if I enjoyed getting booed or clapped more in my career!

I didn't know then, having experienced such joy,

that only a few days later I was to suffer an injury that would finish my rugby career.

March 24th 2006 is a date that will always stick in my mind. We were playing against Glasgow Warriors and I was at the front of a maul when two of their props crashed into me at once and they actually got knocked out. I carried on playing, even though I felt my neck stiffening up. I went to the gym to train the next day, as usual, but I couldn't even pick up a 20-kg dumbbell. It was as if I had no strength at all. I remember thinking that it wasn't a huge searing pain, but I had no strength left.

I went to see the physio and took a week off rugby and weights training, concentrating on my fitness. On the following Sunday, I went to do a weights session and it seemed that my strength had come back so I trained, but when I went home I was in agony! I had horrific headaches and I had to ring the doctor as I was in such pain. I'd known the doctor for ten years and I'd never even asked him for an aspirin. It was totally unlike me to call him so he knew immediately that there must be something very wrong. I was given painkillers and told to meet him in the hospital for a scan at 6.30 a.m. the next morning.

Everything happened very quickly after that. The doctor called mid-afternoon to tell me not to do anything in order to be safe. I had to see a neck surgeon that evening and, half an hour later, I was retired. Easy as that! This was a very tough time for me as I was told that I was one hit away from a wheelchair. My world had changed. I was six weeks from the end of my contract, with the realisation that I had nothing after that. I retired from rugby in 2006 in a way I had never expected. When Cardiff announced that I was no longer going to play for them because of injury, coach Dai Young said, 'He will be sadly missed, I don't know of anybody who doesn't like him – apart from some of the opposition!'

I realise I have been very fortunate in having a successful, if relatively short, career in rugby football. I probably could have won more caps, but had to retire at the age of twenty-seven. I had my fair share of injuries and really couldn't carry on. Despite the fact that I now work (for my dad) rather than play for my living, I can look back with some pride on what I've achieved. Thirty-two Welsh caps, being a member of the World Cup squad and touring with Wales against Argentina and Japan. Yes, I may have made it on to some unenviable lists ... the most yellow cards in one season in England, most yellow cards in a European Cup, and most yellow cards in one season in the Celtic League, but I prefer to look back at the three hundred first-class games I played and the fact that I scored just under a hundred tries: not a bad strike rate for a supposedly 'fat' second row forward.

Being part of the Quinnell family has been the best

thing ever. It can't have been easy for Mum and Dad to bring up three big sons, but they have managed it well. There are always questions about how much we eat. People ask if Mum had to borrow the company van to do the food shopping for the three of us! I will say that when McDonalds first opened in Llanelli, we were taken there as a treat. However, we didn't ask what we could have to eat, we asked, 'How *many* meals can we have?'

I think they did a brilliant job with us. Mum did the shouting while Dad, the calming influence, would just stare. Between them, they instilled strong discipline into our lives. My grandfather, who is ninety-five this year, was my hero growing up. He had really big biceps, so much so that we compared him to Mike Tyson the boxer. As children, he seemed to be huge at five-foot-ten inches tall. Now he seems to have got smaller as we have grown bigger.

As far as my two brothers are concerned, they both, in different ways, have been my inspiration. Scott was, because I wanted to be as good, as fast and as strong as him. To my mind, he was the best player in the world and I just wanted to be like him. From Gavin, I have learnt resilience and the ability to accept whatever life throws at you. Despite what he has gone through, he has remained the nicest person you would ever want to meet and I just hope that some of that niceness has rubbed off on me.

Gramps, Mum and Dad and my two brothers – three generations of inspiration, goodness and love. I have been a very lucky man.

CHAPTER FOUR

Introduction by Lynn Davies
Olympic Gold Medallist – Long Jump

I first met John (JJ) Williams after I had been appointed a physical education lecturer at Cardiff College of Education in Cyncoed. The college was looking to attract new talent and, over the years, established itself as a great centre of sporting excellence. JJ was a student who joined as an extremely promising schoolboy athlete and rugby player. I think at the time he had set his sights on becoming a very good sprinter rather than a rugby player, even though he had excelled at both. He came from a sporting family, and his brother Peter was a very talented triple jumper in his own right.

During his three-year college course, JJ and I worked a lot together and I passed on to him many of the skills and training methods I had learnt from my coach Ron Pickering. He was selected to compete in the 100m and 4x100m relay at the Commonwealth Games held in Edinburgh in 1970. I was also part of that relay team. Running the second leg, I passed the baton on to John, but unfortunately in the end we were pipped on the line by England, just missing out on a bronze medal.

To be selected for your country for the Commonwealth Games is a huge honour for any Welsh athlete, and it would have been interesting to see whether JJ could have gained even more international honours had he stayed in athletics.

We shall never know because, ultimately, he chose rugby as his main sporting focus. His early days on the track, and all those long hours of training as a student at Cyncoed, served him well, and he went on to be one of the very best Welsh and British Lions rugby wing three quarters.

No bronze medal on the track maybe, but on the rugby field his were gold medal performances and I'm very proud to have been part of his early development as a great sportsman.

JJ Williams

*Bridgend RFC, Llanelli RFC, Barbarians, Wales,
British and Irish Lions*

I was born in Nantyffyllon, near Maesteg, the son of
bus driver Glyndwr Albert Williams and the youngest
of four brothers. My older brothers were Terry, Ken
and Peter.

My father would drive the bus from Caerau to
Maesteg every day. He struggled to work full-time
through ill-health, but had to keep going because he
had mouths to feed. He died at the age of sixty when I
was eighteen. I haven't got a lot of boyhood memories
of playing football with him when I was young, I think
because he was too ill. He worked all hours, seven
days a week, which people did in those days to keep
the family going. My mother was a very strong
character and a committed chapel-goer. I, too, went to
chapel regularly until the age of eighteen. Mine was a
very traditional valleys upbringing and I'm proud of it.
It was a wonderful start for a sportsman because the

Llynfi Valley had mountains and fields, ideal for playing plenty of rugby, cricket and soccer. As youngsters, in our mind's eye these fields became famous grounds and we pretended to be our sporting heroes.

I went to Maesteg Comprehensive where, as a schoolboy, I played outside half. Like many others, I also played for the local club Nantyffyllon. Rugby was in my blood from a very early age, but I was a small, spindly boy and got nowhere near an under-15s cap because I was deemed too small. I was lucky enough, though, to have had an excellent PE teacher, David Brown. It was he who introduced me to athletics but, of course, I was also influenced when I was younger by my brother Peter, a Welsh Schools triple jump champion.

At that time, Maesteg school had only just changed to a comprehensive, but its structure was still very much based on the old grammar school system. I wasn't the most academic boy there, but I was in a grammar school stream. On Monday mornings, the first two lessons were Latin. Things didn't get any better, as they were followed by a double period of Chemistry, which I detested. I can't say I enjoyed school life academically, but I enjoyed the sports side of it and, in that regard, my sporting education at Maesteg was excellent. By the age of sixteen or seventeen, I had been selected for the Welsh Schools at outside half. My teammates included JPR Williams, Allan Martin, John Bevan and Keith Hughes, who all went on to be full Welsh internationals – not a bad group!

At the time, I was also the Welsh and British Schools sprint champion. These days, schools tend to be more specialist and pupils excel at one sport or another. When I was growing up, it was quite common to combine sports, and rugby stars such as Ken Jones, DK Jones and Bob Morgan were, as youngsters, all excellent sprint champions and schools rugby internationals. If I had been playing rugby and sprinting at that level today, wealthy rugby clubs in England and France would have been knocking on my dad's door.

In those days the pressure to do well at school was enormous, as well-meaning parents, who hadn't had many opportunities themselves, wanted the very best for their sons and daughters. Education was paramount in the valleys then, and those who became doctors or teachers were well respected in the community. I decided to become a teacher and was lucky enough to gain a place at what is now known as Cardiff Metropolitan University, but at that time was the famous Cardiff College of Education in Cyncoed. It was full of would-be teachers but, luckily for me, it had great athletes and rugby players there as well. It was the ideal education!

RUGBY GENERATIONS

Although I intended to progress at college in the two sports, I was torn between them, thanks to the influence of the rugby and athletics lecturers and coaches. Leighton Davies, in charge of college rugby, told me to concentrate on that game and play for Wales. Olympic gold medallist Lynn Davies, on the other hand, said, 'Your goal should be to represent your country in the Commonwealth Games.' I did combine them both for a while, but then I decided in my last year of college to follow Lynn's advice and chose athletics as the Commonwealth Games was coming up.

I still don't know if that was the right choice, because if I had stuck at rugby I might have gone on the very successful 1971 Lions tour to New Zealand. However, I had made my decision, enjoyed my athletics and I did go to the Commonwealth Games in Edinburgh in 1970.

Wales were never going to win many individual gold medals in track and field, except perhaps for my college lecturer, 'Lynn the Leap' Davies, in the long jump. We did, however, have a very good sprint relay team and had high hopes for a bronze medal. We knew that Jamaica were going to win the gold and that Trinidad and Tobago were going to get silver, but the third place was up for grabs. Terry Davies was our lead-off man, then Lynn Davies, then me and the anchor leg was to be run by Ron Jones, who was the number one sprinter in Great Britain

At all the competitions leading up to the Commonwealth Games we had beaten the other home countries' teams out of sight. We had worked very hard on our baton changes and with quality runners like Ron and Lynn in our team we were really top class. On the morning of the final, Ron Jones dropped out with a knee problem. He was replaced by Howard Davies, a 400m runner and record holder, but he didn't have the blistering pace of a short distance sprinter. Unfortunately, we got beaten on the final straight and came fifth when we definitely should have had the bronze. When I think back on my sporting career and wonder what were my regrets, I always think of the medal that might have been in the Commonwealth Games! Now, whenever I see Ron Jones, who is a fantastic bloke, I pull his leg and never let him forget about it!

I learnt a lot at that Commonwealth Games and I always try to pass on the lessons learnt to my children, who are all athletes. Failure in one competition sometimes helps you become better and stronger at the next. I think you need to go to one, take it all in and learn from it, and then use that experience so that you do better at the next one. That's true in a lot of sports.

Apart from an appearance at the World Student Games in Turin, representing Britain, my time as a serious athletics competitor was coming to an end. I still wanted to be a British international athlete, but first class rugby was also very appealing so I had to make a tough choice. On top of that, I had to concentrate on my career, and having qualified as a teacher, I joined Hartridge School in Newport – my first job.

Although I worked in Newport, I didn't join the Black and Ambers but started playing for Bridgend in 1972. I won an award at the then hugely popular and competitive Snelling Sevens and, after a very enjoyable club tour to Canada, decided that I would finish with athletics and switch to rugby.

Bridgend was a good club, they won championships and were one of the most successful teams in Wales. Despite enjoying my time there, I wasn't progressing as I wanted to. I didn't get selected for the Wales B team or any Welsh squad. I remember playing against Llanelli at Stradey Park one season and they ran us ragged. I looked at their players and thought I'd like to be part of that team with the likes of Phil Bennett and Delme Thomas. Back in the dressing rooms afterwards, I saw the facilities that they had and I consciously made the decision to ring Carwyn James, their coach, and join Llanelli. Chico Hopkins, who had made the decision to go down to Llanelli from Maesteg, also influenced me.

I felt I was on the outside looking in because, at the time, rugby was flying; the very successful 1971 Lions tour had created huge interest in the game. In addition, the returning talented Welsh Lions who were playing for London Welsh were monopolising most of the squad. I was really ambitious and made a massive decision to leave Bridgend and go to Llanelli. Many players at the time didn't venture west, but usually joined Cardiff. I was convinced, however, that my future lay with the Scarlets.

By now, I had a new teaching job as Head of Department at Maesteg Comprehensive, which was a sound career move for me. I was back at my old school; this was really where my heart was and I had great plans to make the school a dominant rugby playing force. It took a few years to achieve, but I did it.

It was a big turning point in my life. My wife Jane and I bought a house in Maesteg and we looked forward to the new challenges. The move to Llanelli rugby club was also a big decision to make, but it was the right one, because now I was rubbing shoulders with Carwyn, Phil and Delme, Derek Quinnell and Tommy David, who had also made the move to Llanelli from Pontypridd.

The larger than life Ray Gravell moved to the centre, a position he made his own for the Scarlets and Wales. Roy Mathias had gone north to play rugby league, so there was a vacancy there for me on the wing.

I didn't go down there with the sole intention of playing against the All Blacks, but when I arrived it was obvious the whole team was gearing itself up for the match against them in the October of 1972. Having been beaten by the Lions, the All Blacks were out for revenge and all the matches we played leading up to the big day were mere stepping stones. The coaching staff, led by Carwyn, included the inimitable Norman Gale, and Tom Hudson, who in his time at Swansea and, later, Bath universities was at the forefront of scientific preparation for rugby matches. He understood the concept of peaking at the right time, much as an athletics coach would do, and used our normal club programme of matches as part of the big build-up for the All Blacks game.

I was selected for the game on the wing with Andy Hill on the other. Andy kicked a penalty, but I didn't have much to do apart from defend. It was a great 9-3 win, a huge triumph for coach Carwyn and captain Delme, and it was the day that the pubs ran dry in Llanelli. The match now forms part of rugby folklore. Thousands and thousands claim to have been there and I'm sure it has been an inspiration for Scarlets teams over the years since.

They were great times at Llanelli. We won the Welsh Cup in front of fifty thousand people and I scored a try. Carwyn's brand of coaching encouraged an expansive, wide game which was brilliant for me because I saw a lot of the ball! More than ever, I was determined to try and break into the Welsh team.

I gained my first cap at the end of the '72-'73 season when I came on as sub against France. I had been playing great rugby in Llanelli, but John Bevan and Gerald Davies were the well-established wingers for Wales. It was unusual for a winger to be chosen for the bench in those days, because only two people were allowed on the field as substitutes, but, as the squad was so depleted with injuries, I got on the field at half-time. We lost 12-3, but I played for the next thirty consecutive games for Wales.

After gaining my first cap, things moved on very quickly. I went on a Wales tour of Canada and scored some good tries. Little did I know that only twelve months into my international career, I would be chosen to represent the 1974 British Lions.

People say in sport that when your moment comes, it can come really quickly. You can be an 'also ran' today and within twelve months the world champion. You have to seize the moment and take it, because it doesn't come often. If you don't, you have no one to blame but yourself.

There also has to be an element of luck. I was lucky enough to get on that tour, lucky to be sub for my first cap, and lucky that there were lots of injuries. At the same time, John Bevan went to rugby league so I went straight into the Welsh team on the left wing for Wales.

I scored some great tries, particularly against Australia and France, that season and I was chosen to go on the 1974 Lions tour to South Africa because of that.

I was confident of being chosen, but other factors helped my selection. Both Gerald Davies and David Duckham said they wouldn't be going so, had I not been selected, I would have been gutted. Carwyn, as always, was very supportive and said that I would make the team. Subsequently, Clive Rowlands, one of the tour selectors, confirmed that mine was one of the first names as a winger on the team sheet. Despite positive assurances, I was still anxious. In those days, you read the *Western Mail* or listened out for news of the squad, and later somebody would phone you to confirm it. It was a matter of fact as that. I first heard I had been picked on the news, just like anybody else would have heard it, and, later that day, a letter came through the letter box saying that I had been chosen. It was a great relief to me because, although I was confident that I would be picked, I wasn't a certainty like Gareth Edwards or JPR Williams.

The tour started a huge debate about apartheid and whether the tour should go ahead. I was still teaching at Maesteg Comprehensive and I began to wonder whether I should go or not. I do remember after school, in training, putting on three wet suits trying to replicate what it would be like playing under a hot sun on the hard grounds of South Africa. Although I knew about and had seen photographs of Nelson Mandela, I hadn't fully realised how politically important his imprisonment on Robben Island was to the apartheid regime.

Politically, Harold Wilson and Ted Heath were vying for power. Wilson said the British Lions shouldn't go while Ted Heath said we should. My employers at the time, the Labour-controlled Mid Glamorgan County Council said that I could go, but wouldn't be paid. Normally, teachers who represent their country would have full leave of absence with pay. In this case, I wouldn't be paid for the four months of the tour, nor for the school holiday period that followed my return, so I had six months without pay. All that fame and no money!

But it didn't matter to me – I was determined to go. For a rugby player, a Lions tour is the pinnacle, it's rugby's Olympic Games. Although my wife, Jane, was teaching at the time, we'd just bought a new house so, financially, it was going to be difficult. We decided that we could just about manage so off I went.

The Welsh players travelled to London by train to meet the rest of the Lions team. Gareth Edwards had said that if you couldn't play rugby in South Africa then you couldn't play anywhere in the world as the conditions were perfect for the game. I've always remembered that. The playing conditions might have been perfect, but the backroom support left a lot to be desired. We played some matches in searing heat and at high altitude, yet no water was provided. At half-time, there were no oranges, and any injury on the field was treated by the local 'rub a dub' man, or sometimes our hooker Ken Kennedy from Ireland, a qualified doctor. There was no entourage of physios and medics then.

I was the quiet, shy boy in the corner having only won six international caps, but I was thrilled and excited to be with these players. Deep down, I was determined to do well on this tour and, if I could, to get in the Test team. We had twenty-two fixtures and I wasn't picked for the first game. In the matches that followed, I didn't play many of the more prestigious Saturday games as I hadn't scored many tries. The reason was simple; the matches were played amongst the forwards, there wasn't much passing of the ball and a lot of the games were just brutal.

It was a tough time, but then we played and won an easy game in a place called Mossel Bay on the coast, ten days before the first Test match, and I scored six tries! I thought, 'I've got to be a leading contender now', but the final Saturday before the first Test we played against Western Province in Cape Town, and again, the selectors didn't pick me and I remember being duty boy.

Instead, I turned out on the Wednesday prior to the Test match against a South African Proteas XV, but I was in good company as my teammates included Fran Cotton, Fergus Slattery and Mervyn Davies. That too was another bruising encounter, but we kept our unbeaten record. On the night of the game, the team was announced for the first Test and I was chosen to play. I couldn't have been happier!

The first Test was held in Cape Town. I remember getting into the dressing room and seeing all the red jerseys hanging up. I looked across the room at our captain Willie John McBride and other household names like JPR Williams, Gareth Edwards and Gordon Brown. I thought, 'This is it; I've made it.' I was now rubbing shoulders with these great players and fulfilling my rugby ambition. I couldn't wait to run down the tunnel and start the match. What I wasn't ready for, however, was the noise. South Africa had been isolated in international sport because of apartheid, so to have the Lions play on home soil was quite something. I thought the Arms Park was loud but it was nothing compared to the cacophony of sound that greeted us from the crowd. Believe it or not, the game was played in torrential rain! It was a total mud bath, and so it was a forwards-orientated match. We won 12-3, but I didn't play particularly well.

The second Test was very different. The spectators were just as noisy but we realised that the black supporters, penned in special enclosures behind the goal posts, were actually applauding all our good play.

It was as if they were glad that someone was getting one over on their white rulers. Having lost the first Test the proud Springboks were under intense pressure to win and had even trained behind closed doors in the grounds of Pretoria jail to get away from the less than happy South African public and press. It didn't do them any good at all. We beat them again and I was fortunate enough to score two beautiful tries, the first British Lions player to score two tries in a Test match.

The third Test in Port Elizabeth was, I suppose, my proudest moment in rugby. We convincingly won the match and I repeated my second Test performance by scoring two more tries. This created a record in itself, as no player before or since has scored four tries in a Test series. They were special tries, the first one in particular when JPR and I switched the ball between us which resulted in me scoring under the posts. I regard this try as one of my best in the Lions shirt.

A draw in the final Test meant we went through the whole tour unbeaten – a remarkable achievement. On a personal level, I scored six tries in one match and four in the Test series, both records that still stand even today. Not bad for someone only twelve months into his international career. As far as this much-publicised tour was concerned, I'm not sure if we were instrumental in bringing an end to apartheid, but I like to think that we made a little bit of a difference, as the previously confident Springboks suddenly found themselves vulnerable, being now subjected again to the pressures of international sport.

Ironically, when I returned from that invincible tour, I was invited to a function at Mid Glamorgan – but I declined! I couldn't stand the hypocrisy, having played all that time without my teaching salary. There were plenty of people who wanted to pat me on the back and share in our success, but didn't realise the sacrifices, financial and otherwise, that we all had to make to play what was, at that time, an amateur sport. Not long afterwards, I left teaching.

I decided to enter the business world as a pharmaceutical rep with, of all people, Clive Rowlands. The selector became my business mentor! I lasted for six months not knowing a dicky bird about the pharmaceutical industry. Clive was the ultimate salesman. We had a great laugh together and would go on courses where we couldn't even pronounce the name of the drug that we were supposed to sell, but miraculously – yet not surprisingly – Clive became one of the top sales reps in the country. He is unique. He has played, coached, managed and been the chairman of selectors for the Welsh team. He is truly the 'Top Cat'!

I continued to play for Llanelli, and we went on to become the Cup Kings of Welsh Rugby, winning four cup finals in consecutive seasons. In fact, the Llanelli team of the mid-seventies won every possible tournament or cup competition that we played in. We followed our great All Blacks victory with another terrific performance, drawing with the touring Australia team of 1975. I scored a lovely try in that game, in a match which we should have won as we were 28-15 up with only minutes to go.

Llanelli was not only victorious in that era but the manner in which we played the game was very special. It was entertainment of the highest order and as a result Stradey Park was packed out for all our games.

But changes are inevitable in sport as in life. The old guard in Llanelli were leaving and at international level Wales needed some new blood, both in the forwards and backs. After a mediocre season in 1974, six new caps were awarded for the first international against France the following year. It was to herald the beginning of another golden age of Welsh rugby as we won four Triple Crowns and two Championships.

For all of this fame, none of us made any fortunes. Amateur rules precluded us from receiving direct payments and although many players were asked to appear in all sorts of TV programmes and advertising campaigns, we were required to pay any money earned back to the Welsh Rugby Union. British Telecom wanted to include the slogan 'All the way with JJ' together with an action picture of myself, as part of their advertising campaign, but this was refused. When I won a heat of the very popular television programme

Superstars, I was presented with the prize money and a TV. I had to return the money, but was told I could keep the television … unfortunately it was a miniature one! It was a different time, with different standards and values.

I went on another Lions tour in 1977 to New Zealand, which was a total contrast to 1974. We went to a country that lived and breathed rugby despite its small size. The men in black are legendary figures and the tour was the toughest test imaginable. To add to my joy as a three quarter, it rained almost non-stop for three months! Despite everything, I loved it because it was my opportunity to prove myself against the very best team in world rugby. There's no such thing as a poor New Zealand rugby player!

We lost the first Test, but won the second in Christchurch. I scored the winning try in that match and I consider it one of my very best because it was against the All Blacks on their home soil. It doesn't come better than that! At one match all, I felt maybe we could win this series, but a pulled muscle after twenty minutes in the third Test meant my contribution to that match and the tour was over. I was devastated.

Whereas South African rugby had suffered from isolation and was not really prepared for the Lions onslaught, in 1974 New Zealand were right on top of their game. They had world-class players like scrum half Sid Going and flanker Ian Kirkpatrick. The All

Blacks were still hurting after being well beaten in 1971 and they were determined to gain revenge. Although you could argue that we were better than them at times, we still lost because, like every other great individual sportsperson or team, they are able to change gear … and win.

In those days, they were fiercely competitive both in attack and defence, you just couldn't score tries against them. These days, although you can score the odd try, they will score more than you – the All Blacks never know when they're beaten, and they seldom are.

I look back at my international rugby career with a deep sense of pride, having been part of very successful Welsh teams. Playing for the Lions was also a great honour. Sadly, all good things must come to an end and, although I played another two seasons for Llanelli, I retired from international rugby after the game against England in 1979. We won 27-3 and I also scored a try – it was good to go out on a high!

Naturally, there were a few regrets because I had enjoyed my time very much, but the reality was that I'd had sixteen years of non-stop sport and training … and I was getting slightly slower. I suppose if I were playing now, I would have gone on another five years, but in those days I had to go to find work, pay my mortgage and feed my family. I became self-employed and set up my own painting company. Now there were new challenges ahead and, as ever, I was prepared to throw everything into it. I suppose I approached business in the same way as I approached my sport – with hard graft. It's a philosophy I still hold after all these years in business, but the whole experience has been tremendously satisfying.

* * *

Looking back, I think I could have achieved more if I'd had the benefit of modern day sports science and good advice around me. I lost my father at a young age and then later my mother passed away which made me feel very isolated. I hope that I have given my children every encouragement and support and I hope it's made a difference to their lives.

It has been interesting to see how my three children have reacted so differently to any advice I've been able to give over the years. I have coached them, but not officially. James didn't like it … Kathryn thrived on it and Rhys, who was a very promising rugby player early on, didn't want to be seen up in Loughborough being guided by his dad – he wanted to choose his own coach. Athletics is such a lonely sport and I've always maintained that to succeed you need a good team around you. Athletes can also be very selfish in their drive for individual success. In rugby you have to be a team player first and foremost.

I'm very proud of all three of my children. They all tried a number of sports before settling on what they really liked. I'm glad that Jane and I taxied them all around the country and supported them financially – we've had fun together, sharing the highs and lows of competitive sport with them! Were they under more pressure because of my success? I don't think so, but they've handled everything that's come their way very well.

As I reflect on my rugby career, I do wonder what will happen in the future to our national team. The game has changed enormously over the last twenty years – I don't recognise much of it now. My hope is that today's players will enjoy the game as much as we did. As in all professional sport, money is the real driving force nowadays and other sports will come to rival rugby for the attention of the Welsh nation. Rugby in Wales has always been a great game, played with flair and passion. May that continue for future generations.

CHAPTER FIVE

Introduction by Adrian Thomas
Cefn Cribwr RFC, Maesteg RFC, GB National Athletics Coach

It can be very difficult for a young man or woman interested in making a career in sport to follow their dream when either or both their parents are famous sports personalities in their own right. When a shy young man came to me seventeen years ago, I realised that he had the potential to be a great athlete, but in Wales he would always be known as the son of rugby legend JJ Williams.

Rhys Williams first approached me in 1999, determined to be a successful 400m hurdler, having already made his name at a young age as a very promising swimmer and rugby player. He was in good company, as the group I coached then included Daniel Caines (World Indoor 400m Champion) and Mark Rowlands (World/European Under-20 4x400m bronze medallist). Rhys was inspired and motivated by those athletes' success and after two years of training and working extremely hard he won the European Youth Olympic title. This was the first of his four European titles, and he was probably the only athlete to have won the whole set.

In 2001, I retired from coaching and over the next few years, Rhys trained with others and established himself as a top class athlete. We joined forces again twelve years later and his consistent forty-eight-second performances in the 400m hurdles ranked him in the world top twenty athletes in 2013.

The next few years proved extremely difficult for Rhys. The joy of being selected as captain of Wales at the Commonwealth Games in Glasgow was counterbalanced by the disappointment at not being selected for the Olympic Games in Rio. This was despite having run the necessary qualifying times on two occasions and being the only athlete to make the 2016 European Championship 400m hurdle final.

Rhys's outstanding quality, though, is that he never gives up. He has enormous belief in his own ability and is still prepared to work and train hard to achieve his goals. He now has his sights set on competing at the World Championships in London in 2017 and wearing the red vest of Wales again at the Commonwealth Games in 2018.

Would Rhys have made a great rugby player?

Evidence suggests yes he would. His father JJ Williams, Nigel Walker, Allan Martin and Brynmor Williams are examples of those who made successful transitions from athletics to rugby. If attitude, professionalism and determination were enough, Rhys definitely could have joined them, but having chosen athletics we will never know.

Rhys Williams

European Championships – Gold, Silver and Bronze
Medallist, 400m hurdles

Growing up, did I realise that my dad was famous? Not at all … to me, he was just my dad. Although he had won countless trophies and had many jerseys from countries he had played against, they were never really on show. It was home, not a sports museum – although I did imagine myself wearing the red jersey of Wales. As I grew up though, despite having seen old videos of Dad in action, I began to notice that when he took me to rugby matches, people would stop him to ask for his autograph and enthuse about his great tries and his speed as 'The Welsh Whippet' on the rugby pitch. They seemed to know so much about him and I was proud to hear them praising *my* dad. It became clear that he was fairly well known in Wales!

Although I might have taken Dad's fame for granted, I was definitely in awe of the players who visited our house regularly. Who could not be impressed when Gareth Edwards, JPR, Phil Bennett and Robert Jones dropped by?

I would be lying if I said that sport didn't come easy. As a young boy I was always active; I remember playing rugby with Dad in the fields around Porthcawl and I also liked to play with his old starting blocks and spikes, so rugby and athletics were a big influence right from the start. My parents were great with us all – James, Kathryn and me – encouraging us and letting us try all kinds of sports. Although Dad taught me the basics, I never felt he pushed me into anything and I was grateful for that. I was really pleased though when he came to my primary school and took a rugby session – even the PE teachers took notice of what he said, and I was proud of that.

When I began playing rugby myself, I wasn't quite so pleased. I noticed that every time I got the ball I would have about five people marking me, so I had a lot to thank my dad for in that respect! Despite having inherited Dad's speed, and to an extent his mental robustness, I was a real target on the pitch. To be the son of JJ Williams meant they expected a lot from me and I expected a lot of myself too. To hear some of the parents watching point me out and say, 'That's JJ's son,' was great on one hand, but did add just a little pressure.

I was quite hard on myself, even from an early age, but I like to think that in my case rugby's loss was athletics' gain! Apart from my father who made the switch, I also remember seeing Tom James, a very talented 800m runner, who went on to represent Wales, training hard on the sand dunes at Mynydd Mawr. These small mountains of pain have attracted countless athletes and sportsmen and women from other disciplines to train there. It must have paid off for Tom, because when he gave up athletics he went on to play rugby on the wing with great distinction for Cardiff Blues and Wales.

I've always said I've never been the most talented boy in the school but I always worked the hardest. I would train the hardest, and I'd be more committed than any of my peers. I'd keep at it, determined to give a hundred per cent to whatever sport I was participating in. I tried hard and kept going, always believing that by concentrating and refusing to give in, I could make myself stronger and fitter and quicker. I would never give up and Dad would always be there to help with that.

My whole family is really sporty. It's a good job really that my mum loves sport too. My brother and sister were very talented and competed for their country long before me. James was a 1500m runner and Kathryn a 400m hurdler and they have continued their association with athletics in their working lives. I didn't get into the sport until much later so I was always looking up to them and I worked hard to be as good as they were, which must have helped. We've always cheered one another on and been supportive in whatever sport we are competing in.

It must have been hard for Dad to stop himself coaching us all from the sidelines. He wasn't always able to help himself, but we realised that his advice was worth hearing. He gave us good input about our progress and his feedback, though sometimes hard to take, was right. I think I leaned on him too much when I was younger, sometimes to my own disadvantage. I've had to learn to follow my own path in sport.

I had an excellent grounding in Ysgol y Ferch O'r Sger Primary School, Bridgend. Mr Mason was a great sports teacher and, more importantly, a great motivator. He really believed in his pupils' potential and got the best out of us. My first big event was a cross-country race in junior school when I was about ten years old. I remember there was a favourite to win the race and I beat him, even though I hadn't trained for it. That first taste of success was wonderful and it had come relatively easily.

I then went to Ysgol Llanhari, a Welsh medium school in Rhondda Cynon Taf, where Iolo Roberts was my sports teacher. He, like Mr Mason, was hugely inspirational. He taught rugby during the winter and coached us in athletics in the summer months. He let us enjoy sport first of all, and I am grateful to him for how he encouraged us. I still feel indebted to him and I am proud now to consider him a good friend.

RHYS WILLIAMS

I was always first in school races and the fastest in my class; I have happy memories of sports days at school, lining up against the others and twitching as I waited for the shout of 'Go'! I wanted to win and I wanted to make my parents proud as they watched with all of the other parents. I knew some of my friends were quick, but I was determined to beat them and win the race. I loved that first-time experience of a crowd shouting your name. It spurred me on!

I've always been grateful that I have inherited good sporting genes, but I realised there are always people who've got more inherent talent. It's how you choose to use it that's important. Many of those people never fulfil their obvious potential because they don't possess the necessary work ethic and 1 was determined from a very young age always to be prepared to keep trying, which I was convinced would bring benefits in the long run.

I wasn't one of those people who was brilliant at all sports though. I'd shy away from the sports that needed specific skills, like golf and cricket, because I wasn't good in that way, but sports that involved running and maybe a bit of ability, power and strength, I did really well in.

I was picked for the school basketball and rugby teams; football wasn't an option at school. I was a member of the Bridgend and District DC Thomas winning rugby side at the age of eleven. I joined my excited teammates to travel on the bus to the capital and was fortunate to play in such an iconic stadium on a beautiful day and in front of such a large crowd. Before the game, we had a very inspirational team talk reminding us what a great honour it was to run out on the field that had seen such great rugby encounters over the years. It was quite heavy stuff for under-11s, but I loved every minute of it. The son of JJ got to play at Cardiff Arms Park after all! On the day in question, Dad was commentating for BBC Wales on the game ... not the DC Thomas cup, but the Welsh Cup Final that followed immediately after our curtain raiser!

In the summer, the school did athletics and I really enjoyed it. Today there is so much more choice of sports in school, but then things were very traditional and more limited. I did a lot of swimming and it became my priority at one time. I enjoyed it and made a lot of good friends in the sport. I was chosen to swim for Wales and I became the Welsh under-15 backstroke champion. Again, I have a lot to thank my parents for, as they would take me to swimming classes at unearthly hours, often nine times a week, and support me in whatever I did. I gave it my all as I wanted to be good at it; I was determined to succeed and went at it full pelt. It was great cardiovascular training and, because it's not a weight bearing sport, worked well alongside my athletics preparation. It was a very happy time training at the local pool in Pyle, near Bridgend, and I had numerous coaches who were all very generous with their time and advice and encouraged us all the way.

One of the girl swimmers there was a Commonwealth Games contender, Gemma Howells, and it was great training alongside her because she was really committed. I learnt a lot from watching her and trying to emulate her dedication. There were other really talented athletes there, as well, like triathletes Helen Tucker (later Jenkins) and Marc Jenkins. Marc is still one of my heroes, as he would never give up, which he proved much later in the 2004 Olympics – his bike was damaged and unusable in the cycling leg but, rather than quitting because he was last, he carried it on his shoulders to finish the race to tumultuous applause from the crowd. Marc and his wife Helen demonstrate what sport is really about to me and I have the utmost respect for them. They are both champions in my eyes.

Marc used to train like a maniac – he was the hardest trainer I've ever seen! I always wanted to be focused like that. We spurred one another on and his attitude to hard work was one that I have always thought about when the going got tough in my own training.

As I got older, swimming ceased to have the appeal it once had. I didn't make the Welsh Schools swimming team and on a school skiing trip made what would turn out to be a life-changing decision to concentrate solely on athletics.

I quickly gained a Welsh Schools vest, confirming that my decision was the right one. Although I didn't realise it at the time, athletics was also going to help me find my future wife: Leila, an 800m runner, trained with my brother and ran for Welsh schools. I always liked her but was too shy to talk to her. Leila was thirteen and I was fifteen.

* * *

I left school at eighteen after achieving A levels in PE, RE, History and an A/S in Biology, and went to study a degree in Sports Science and Management at Loughborough University. Dad encouraged me to go to college to ensure I had a breadth of sports knowledge. It was my first choice as the university has an international reputation for excellence in sport science. I wanted to learn from the best. I loved being part of such a dynamic and forward-looking sports department, learning new disciplines to help my career in the future as well as my immediate sporting needs. It was a huge campus university and the calibre of athletes there was amazing. I remember being in awe when I arrived and wanting to learn as much as I could from those who were already well known. My first impression of the college was that all the best people in sport were students there! Among them were Commonwealth medallist Kamel Thompson from

Jamaica, British 400m runner Sean Baldock and Paralympic champion, Dan Greaves.

Iwan Thomas, the Welsh 400m runner, and Chris Rawlinson, the 400m hurdler, were also training there and I was way off the pace compared to them at that time and had a lot to learn. Iwan became a good friend and mentor, giving me advice and helping when I needed support. I looked up to him and aspired to be like him. I respected his relentless determination and hard work, but he was great fun too. His later medal haul in the Olympic Games, the European Championships and World Championships confirmed his outstanding talent, demonstrated from a young age.

University was a positive experience for me. I learnt about time management, being honest enough to recognise where I needed to improve. I was hard on myself in the first year, thinking that I was useless, as I battled between trying to work hard, trying to train hard and trying to socialise. I competed in Loughborough and my first British vest was for the British Junior team coached by Nick Dakin. Each year there was a Loughborough International meet against GB Juniors and I was competing against twenty-four- or twenty-five-year-old athletes. I didn't win, but I got a personal best, did myself justice and I was proud of my achievement. My 400m hurdles career was on the way.

Now, looking back, I recognise that, having won a

number of European medals, my time management couldn't have been that bad. It was a huge learning curve for me and I enjoyed the challenge and realised it was good life experience. I was European Youth Champion in 2001, European Junior Champion in 2003 and European Under-23 Champion in 2005.

That year, I got the selection letter to join the British senior team. It was a great step up. I was ranked in the first two, running good times, and my coach gave me confidence to hope that I'd be selected. It was fantastic to get the call-up and I remember how great I felt.

By the end of my three years in university, my confidence had grown and I felt on par with the others. I began a Master's degree in Marketing, only too aware even then that I needed to prepare for a life after athletics. My degree was part-time, as I was trying to go from being a junior athlete to a senior competing athlete. Unfortunately, I had a lot of injuries at that time which hampered me in many ways. Halfway through the course, I came home from Loughborough to Cardiff and finished my Master's Degree at the University of Glamorgan.

* * *

In 2006, I came fourth in the Commonwealth Games in Melbourne, setting a new Welsh record. I had run three races, heats, the semi-final and the final and did a personal best in every round. My finishing time would have won gold four years later but, even with a national record, I still didn't get a medal. Despite good performances and results, one of my lowest points came in that year. I had four stress fractures and a toe operation and at one stage seriously thought I might never run again – it was a nightmare. I went from running well to being unable to run at all. I didn't feel like an athlete any more as I couldn't even jog!

Again, it was the lessons learnt about discipline and determination in my early days that got me through this tough time. I had to undergo a strict programme of rehabilitation and long, lonely hours in the gym and on the track before I got back to anything approaching my previous levels of fitness and performance. As 'the forgotten man of British Athletics' – a tag that hurt – I was dropped from Lottery funding and had it not been for my parents' support again, I would never have been able to make any sort of comeback. It made me more determined than ever to repay them in some way.

In my senior career, I have won European Championships bronze, silver and gold medals in my event and a silver medal in the 4x400m relay. Looking back, that race reminded me a little of my time playing rugby. Although individual performances are vital in a relay, if the team doesn't gel and get the baton around, the team loses. Our team that day performed well and I will always be grateful to Robert Tobin, Graham Hedman and Tim Benjamin; our silver medal was well-deserved.

These bare facts hide hours and hours of training and preparation in readiness for the big event. Race days for me follow a well-established pattern. The night before, I make sure to have an early night and often have messages of support from family and friends. I appreciate these very much but I'm not sure that Dad's advice, 'This is your race to lose', just before the 2012 European Championships in Helsinki did much for my nerves!

On race day morning, I have breakfast, do a short warm-up, then relax in my room by reading or watching television. I get a light lunch, go for a short walk, grab a little sleep, go to the track and I'm ready to race. Opponents over the years have always tried little tricks in the warm-up area and on the start line to try and put others off. Some seem to enjoy running directly at you so that you have to move out of the way. Others try to catch your eye just to distract you. I suppose it's to establish some early supremacy, but I'm well used to these games now! I tell myself if they're resorting to that, then they're obviously worried about me. Any advantage I have is bound to help!

* * *

I am proud to have represented Wales in the Commonwealth Games in Delhi in 2010 where I gained a bronze medal. As I went down to the start of that race, there were bugs everywhere and as I prepared to get on my blocks, I was somewhat distracted by a large grasshopper by my right hand. As I do in every race, I touched my lobes and the gun went off. I never saw the grasshopper again, but I did get a medal!

As a proud, Welsh-speaking Welshman, wearing the red vest has always meant the world to me. For my dad, scoring tries and playing well for Wales was equally important. I was always determined to give my very best in every race I entered. Sport teaches you to win and to lose and I'm glad that my family have been there for me at every stage. They have travelled to competitions around the world to cheer me on. In televised events, the camera has frequently picked out Dad in the crowd, and commentators invariably say, 'There's JJ Williams, one of the great Welsh rugby legends and ... Rhys's father.' After races, Mum and Dad have joined me in the team hotel ready to commiserate or congratulate – they have always been very supportive and have taken an active interest in every stage of my athletics career – the good times and the bad.

In 2014 I was chosen to be captain of the Welsh team at the Commonwealth Games in Glasgow. It was one of the proudest moments of my life. My dad was thrilled for me, understanding so well how I felt. I gave the team speech in the holding camp in Portugal, in no doubt that this was the highlight of my career. I went to bed thinking that I had done a good job to raise the team's game. The next day I was told that another Welsh athlete and I had failed a drug test and would be sent home. I was devastated and entirely innocent. The supplement we had taken had a verification certificate and we were completely in shock to hear of any hint of wrongdoing. I was shattered by the whole awful experience. The supplements I was taking were on the agreed list. The contamination had occurred in the factory and would have been impossible to detect because of its miniscule presence, and therefore impossible for me to know anything about.

Coming home with my coach, Adrian Thomas, it was as if someone had died; I'd worked hard, been a total sports professional but my reputation felt ruined. Adrian was my first major coach, knew me from a young age and really understood me. He has always known what makes me tick. He is a genuinely nice guy and I respect him absolutely as a coach. He still looks after me when I haven't done well and pushes me when I need to do better.

I couldn't speak on the plane, going over and over in my head what might have happened. My dad was entirely supportive and behind me every step of the way to clear my name. It was an expensive and long process to prove my innocence and uphold the family honour. I hadn't cheated and I didn't want Dad's name and my name tarnished by the tabloids. We have stuck together and worked hard to ensure that the charge was dismissed and my name cleared.

Although 2015 was difficult and I was extremely disappointed not to be selected for the Olympics in Rio, I was proud and somewhat vindicated to have been awarded Welsh Athlete of the Year 2016 by the Welsh Athletics governing body, the second time I have won this award. I have to be positive and look to the future. I still feel I am capable of running good races and setting good times. If not, I can still look back on my career with some pleasure and satisfaction.

Dad was the best. I've always been proud of him. I hope I have made him proud of me too.

CHAPTER SIX

Introduction by Nigel Walker
Cardiff RFC, Wales

Class – that's the one word I would use to describe Mark Ring as a rugby player. I first met Mark when we played for Cardiff Schools under-11s in 1973! While I was simply delighted to be part of the final squad, Mark was totally determined to shine and to let his skills and use of the ball impress all those around him; he was head and shoulders above every other player, in terms of ambition, confidence and ball skills. I played against him for many years as I represented Rumney High School and he Lady Mary's High School. After leaving school, it would be a full eleven years before our paths crossed again.

In the intervening years, I had witnessed the growth of an absolutely world-class player as he plied his trade with Cardiff and, of course, Wales. Thirty-two caps he won for Wales, which is a meagre return for a player of his ability, and below the number he should have accumulated were it not for the wretched knee injuries he sustained when he should have been in his prime.

When I returned to rugby in 1992, and played alongside him for Cardiff, he may have lost half a yard of pace but his rugby brain was still razor sharp: his eye for the gap, and his ability to spot weaknesses in our opponents' defences, was simply on a different level to his peers. He had all the silky skills and could show off with the best of them, such as when he back-heeled a conversion during a competitive match, which resulted in a severe telling-off from the powers that be. He was not just outrageously gifted in attack, he was a courageous and tenacious defender too – literally the complete package.

The game that summed up Mark's brilliance and ability to entertain was the France v Wales game in 1985. Wales lost the game 14-3, but it was lit up by two or three clean breaks by Mark in a game where, apart from that, Wales did not threaten.

I played with and against some great players in my six years in the senior game, but none could match the vision and brilliance of Mark Ring. Truly a class apart and certainly the best Welsh player of his generation.

Mark Gerarde Ring

Cardiff RFC, Pontypool RFC, Wales

My name is Mark Ring. I could have been named Gerarde as my mother wanted, but my nan intervened, so it's now my middle name and I'm proud of it. I was born in the Cardiff district of Splott into a Catholic family, and when my mother was in the maternity hospital, my nan called to see her, wearing a pendant of St Gerarde Majella, the Italian patron saint of expectant mothers.

My mother and father came from large families. My mother, Christine Mary O'Reilly, had five sisters and two brothers and my father four brothers and two sisters, but my parents only had three children, my brother Paul, my sister Carmel and me, the eldest.

My dad, Brian, was probably my greatest influence when it came to sport. Although a Cardiff boy who had stints playing with Canton, St Albans and Old Illtydians, he moved to join the police force in the Midlands. He played for the famous Leicester Tigers between 1959 and 1961 (before I was born) and one of his teammates was the legendary AJF (Tony) O'Reilly, who not only played with great distinction for the Barbarians, Ireland and the British Lions, but went on as the only non-American President of Heinz to be one of Ireland's wealthiest businessmen. Dad was an excellent all round sportsman who played football, rugby, cricket and baseball. Watching him play made me so proud. I like to think that some of his talent rubbed off on me. Although past his prime when I saw him play, two things stand out vividly in my memory. One was a drop goal from the halfway line at Llandaff rugby club, and the other a dummy the like of which I've never seen before or since, where seemingly the whole opposing team went one way and Dad the other. He still had it! To this day, I relive his sporting glories, as I have boxes of his old press cuttings and can spend hours reading them.

I went to St Albans Primary School and then Lady Mary High School in Cardiff. As was the tradition in Catholic schools, I played rugby in the winter and baseball in the summer. It seemed that cricket was what the Protestant schools played in the summer months then. In both my schools, I enjoyed a number of sports and even had cricket trials at Sophia Gardens – Dad told me I was more talented at cricket than anything else and I enjoyed practising with him at weekends.

MARK GERARDE RING

One of my earliest sporting memories was the Nazareth House Sports Day held at Blackweir Fields in Cardiff and attended by all the Catholic schools in the area. My main event that day was the egg and spoon race. Having gone through with difficulty in the preliminary rounds, I made the final and, to my absolute delight, managed to win. The prize was a large, cut-glass punch bowl on a silver-plated base – my first sports trophy. I carried it home proudly and even to this day, my mother has it on prominent display.

I did OK at school. At St Albans, I remember one teacher in particular, Mr Austin Camp. He was real 'old-school', dressed in a formal, black suit with hair to match, and he wore a pocket watch, which fascinated me. He was very strict, but very good and once told my mum that he was convinced that I would go on to good things in my academic career. He would take us, aged ten, into the hall with a pencil and a blank sheet of paper and put on long playing records of Elgar's *Sea Pictures*, Vaughan Williams's *Symphony No 5* or music by Mozart, Sibelius and Beethoven. He would then give us a quick résumé of what the music was about and we'd have to write our thoughts down. He was an unbelievable teacher to fire our imagination in that way and at that age, and I will never forget it.

Another primary school teacher who was a huge influence was Mr Leek, the sports teacher. He was from St Helens originally and had played rugby league. What he was doing in Cardiff I don't know, but I'm glad he was there. In those days, it was commonplace for teachers to stay on after school and arrange games on Saturday mornings and I loved every minute of it.

We travelled on two buses, taking a bus from Newport Road into town, then another out to Holy Family in Fairwater, or out to Llanrumney, to play a team like St Cadoc's. We wouldn't think twice about it and got the same two buses home. Mr Leek would accompany us there and make sure we got home safely, counting us out and counting us back.

He was a big man, weighing about fourteen and a half stones, but he insisted that even as a seven-year-old I had to tackle him. It was frightening, but I learnt how to do the right thing at an early age. One of the key learning stages for children, I believe, is seven to eleven years old and Mr Leek knew that. Sixteen or seventeen years of age is too late to teach a kid to tackle and sidestep.

From the headmaster, Mr John Harrington, through to all the teachers, rugby football in St Albans was very important and there were close links between the school and St Albans RFC who enjoyed the nickname 'The Buns'. For every game the school won, the team was treated to lovely jam-filled cream buns from Janet's pantry in Splott, courtesy of Mr George Daniels. Mr Harrington also entrusted me with the captaincy of both baseball and rugby teams. Although that, in itself, would have been enough, additionally I was also chief selector. Imagine being given that degree of responsibility at such a young age. It was quite remarkable really. I decided very quickly, though, that I would consult others in my age group about the merits of various players, which, in turn, was a great way of creating team spirit, togetherness and camaraderie.

* * *

Junior school also gave me my first taste of baseball. Although generally confined to Cardiff and Newport in Wales, the game was extremely popular and demanded a high level of hand/eye co-ordination, something that served me well later in my rugby career. Midweek and weekend baseball games attracted lots of teams and their supporters to parks around these cities. In England, Liverpool was the hub of baseball; I suppose the game had grown because dockers played it. I well remember staying with other Catholic families during baseball trips and my first journey northwards was at the age of ten, which was quite an experience. It was always something to look forward to and made me better prepared for sporting journeys to come.

I played baseball for three clubs in Cardiff in later years, St Peter's, Old Illtydians and Grange Albion. I was fortunate enough to win four Welsh caps, one of only four Welsh rugby internationals to have represented their country at baseball. One of these was Pontypool and Wales scrum half David Bishop, a fierce competitor, and I'll never forget one occasion when my teammate and good friend slapped me across the face telling me I was far too laid back and that I should treat the game with respect when representing my country. He was a great motivator and he was right!

After junior school, I should have gone to St Illtyd's School with all my mates. There, boys from St Cadoc's, St Albans, Blessed John Lloyd and De La Salle all merged together. My parents, though, had moved house, which meant that it was easier to get me to Lady Mary High School, which comprised pupils from Christ the King, St Joseph's and St Peter's schools. Initially, I wasn't happy at this move and felt like an outsider, but I knew the best sports guys through playing rugby, as I was Cardiff School Boys captain. Jonathan Taylor was a brilliant schoolboy scrum half, but decided not to pursue the game in later life. Other classmates were Adrian Hadley, Michael Budd and Martin Daly, who remains a great friend to this day. All of us went on to play for Cardiff RFC and some for Wales.

Playing schoolboy rugby also gave me my first taste of touring and travel. We went on a regular basis to Pembroke, Ireland and Brussels by coach and boat. Inevitably there would be a great deal of singing, impromptu card schools and that first sneaky pint of beer – all part of growing up!

One of my main problems in those early days was that I was considered too small. Although I had played for Cardiff Boys and had had schoolboy trials at a young age, I still couldn't break through into more representative rugby which, at that time, I found hard to understand. I remember playing against Neath schools and we won 40-0. I must have scored two tries, and kicked all the conversions, a drop goal and penalties. The boy that I played against was the under-15s capped player, the incumbent in my position, so it was hard for me to get a look in. The following year was the under-16s trials and forty boys were invited to a three-day camp in Aberystwyth. The selectors released two players and I was one of them. What a disappointment! My dad always reminded me that it was a long journey home from Aberystwyth and that I'd cried all the way home. I had put a lot into it and didn't get anything out of it – a bitter blow at the time!

* * *

I left school and worked as a civil servant at Companies House in the Department of Trade and Industry. I also grew in height and put on weight and played ninety-nine games for an undefeated Cardiff Youth team. I was then invited to be a reserve in a trial for the Cardiff and District Youth team where I met my great friend and fellow player for many years, Glenn

Webbe. As luck would have it, the Whites fly half didn't turn up, so I was promoted into his place. At half-time, the supposed reserve side, the Whites, with me included, were beating the Reds so I was moved to that team and, from then on, became the Welsh Youth fly half.

Looking back, I think I was very fortunate that the original Whites fly half didn't show up, otherwise I would have had limited game time and might well not have made the final team. Although there was quite a complicated system of selection and trials in those days, I firmly believed that if you were good enough you would get in eventually, whatever your background. A Cardiff Arms Park favourite, Gerald Cordle, was primarily a soccer player from Butetown. He turned up to the Cardiff trials where nobody had heard of him or seen him play. He scored three great tries and became a regular first team player on the wing.

Another wing who I had played with at youth level was Nigel Walker. Blessed with great pace, he decided to concentrate on athletics and reached the semi-finals of the 110m hurdles in the Los Angeles Olympic Games. After the disappointment of not making the final, I asked him whether he would consider coming back to rugby and introduced him to the then Cardiff Director of Rugby, Alec Evans. Alec's first question to Nigel was, 'How fast can you run the 100m?' Nigel told him 10.7 seconds, and, without hesitation, Alec turned to me and said, 'We'll take him!' Nigel went on to play over a hundred games for Cardiff and gained seventeen caps for Wales. Athletics' loss was certainly rugby's gain!

In those days, the logical next step for a youth player would be to play for Cardiff's second team, known affectionately as the Rags. In that pre-professional era, all financial resources were spent on running the two teams and the Rags was a lovely combination of youngsters coming in and older players dropping down so there was a perfect mix – a blend of youth exuberance and experience. In the off-season, my mates and I went to Maindy stadium in our spare time. We did a lot of core work and high intensity training, and practised speed work on the track, to bridge the gap between an under-developed youth player and a seasoned first team regular. I got my Rags cap in my first year as a senior player – quite an achievement!

I played one game for Cardiff as a substitute while I was officially still a youth player. I had played the Youth Cup Final against Newport in Caerphilly on the last Wednesday of the season and, on the following day, Cardiff first team went on a mini tour to play Côte Des Basques in Biarritz. They took me, a rookie, on the senior tour. It was great; I was on a rugby tour! I hadn't been subjected to drink before and I certainly hadn't drunk the amount of alcohol they consumed. On one boozy night out, luckily, I was found behind one of the curtains in a nightclub by one of our players, Bobby Newman, a schoolteacher who spoke fluent French. I was saved and taken back to the hotel at six o'clock in the morning. I survived the initiation and, after that, the players took me under their wing. The following day, I played against Serge Blanco, a young winger then, not a full back. He scored three tries that day and we were well beaten. Nobody knew him at the time. He was electrifying: so much pace and full of confidence. Every time he had the ball, the whole crowd roared. He was one of those dream players who light up the game and get you on the edge of your seat.

* * *

My rise to international rugby was very quick: 1980-81, Welsh Youth cap; '81-'82, first year at Cardiff; and '82-'83 my first cap for Wales against the old enemy, England. Originally, I wasn't selected, but Robert Ackerman from Newport broke his thumb in training, so the WRU phoned my dad and told him to get me ready. That was the only game I played that season in the Five Nations Championship because Robert was declared fit for the other games. I wasn't upset about this, just grateful that the selectors had realised that there was an up-and-coming player (me) ready to step into the breach.

As always, there was huge expectation and a big

build-up before the game against England at home. I was rooming with Terry Holmes, the Cardiff scrum half, although I was going to play at centre. Terry tried to calm my nerves and told me to savour every moment because the eighty minutes would go by in a flash. He was right – that's exactly how it was!

I was one of five new caps that day: Malcolm Dacey replacing Gareth Davies at outside half, Mark Wyatt coming in at full back, with hooker Billy James and flanker David Pickering joining the Welsh pack. The team was captained by Eddie Butler, but I have to say it was a massively disappointing game from my perspective, although we drew 13-13. I touched the ball four times and sensed that some of the senior players were hiding me, looking after me in a way. This, to me, was very frustrating as I desperately wanted the ball and, despite it being my first cap, I had a lot of confidence in my own ability. To this day I'm convinced that if Terry Holmes had passed me the ball in the dying minutes I would have dropped a goal and won the match for Wales. It never happened, but I can still dream!

My memories of our Triple Crown match against England in 1988 were much better. In those pre-social-media days, expressions of good luck came in the form of telemessages. There were about ten for us in our dressing room and I couldn't resist opening one. It said simply, 'Kick holy s**t into the English', signed Spike

Milligan! Now, I wish I'd kept that for myself – an amazing memento of a great day.

For this game, my first at Twickenham, the selectors picked four outside halves: Tony Clement from Swansea was at full back, captain Bleddyn Bowen from South Wales Police and myself, then at Pontypool, were in the centre, and Jonathan (Jiffy) Davies, from Llanelli, was the actual outside half. Jiffy was at his confident and cheeky best. England had picked Mickey Skinner as open-side flanker to put the Welsh team under pressure and to generally make a nuisance of himself. From the first scrum, however, Jiffy shouted, in the direction of the England scrum, 'Mickey, Mickey … Which way am I going?' This continued all through the match, but the taunting worked, as 'Mickey the Munch' never laid a finger on him! His confidence spread to the whole team, Adrian Hadley scored two great tries, and we beat the English at Twickenham by 11-3.

As was the tradition later, both teams met up in a London hotel for the official dinner and after-match function. We were 'forced' to listen to some worthy speeches and grudging congratulations from the opposition, but Glenn Webbe, in his usual fashion, had decided to liven up proceedings. He had brought with him a pink, plastic box. When you pulled a cord at the end of the box, it made a noise like a rent-a-crowd with cries of, 'Bravo! Bravo!' and vigorous clapping accompaniment. The losing captain, Mike Harrison, who in his speech was desperately trying to make the best of the situation, didn't stand a chance! After he had tried to crack a few jokes that went down like lead balloons and were greeted with stony silence, the room was suddenly filled with shouts of, 'Bravo! Bravo!' and tumultuous clapping. Webby's plastic box intervention had been timed to perfection. Everything went quiet again but, not content with one interruption, Webby pulled the cord again ... and again ... and again! Those who didn't know at first where this noise was coming from had now sussed out who the culprit was. Had Webby not repeated the joke, everything would have been OK, but Mickey Skinner had had enough and from a nearby table the atmosphere started to change and someone started throwing gateaux. He came across to our table, snatched the box from Webby and tried to smash it. Unfortunately for him, it was made of hard plastic, wouldn't break and just kept being set off and making 'Bravo' and clapping noises all the time. Finally, in his anger, he just threw Webby's box into a carafe of wine and made his way back to his own table.

Quietly, Webby stood up, calmly rolled up his sleeves, pulled the box out of the wine, gave it a wipe, pulled the cord and it just went 'bloop, bloop'. It was wrecked and dead. Webby was very unhappy that his precious clapping box had been irretrievably damaged in such a manner, so he and Mickey Skinner started eyeballing one another. I could sense that something was going to happen. The seating plan that night was English player, Welsh player alternately and I was next but one to my mate as usual and, so, in the thick of all this action. By now, Webby had called Mickey to go outside and Skinner had left the table with an English player; he'd needed no persuasion to go outside.

I followed my good friend and realised suddenly that three or four English players had now come out to support Mickey Skinner, together with a reporter who was at the dinner. Webby had by now taken his blazer off but we were hopelessly outnumbered, Webby and I against four of England's finest! In this potential mayhem, I was able to warn my friend to be careful because of the all-seeing reporter watching our every move. Glenn Webbe's response was magnificent. Instead of fighting, he challenged Mickey the Munch to an arm wrestling bout. Right arm, left arm, again and again – it was no contest. The winger destroyed the flanker as Jiffy had destroyed him on the field of play. Wales had won again!

Surprisingly enough, Webbe the arm wrestler had had enough of the dinner and the officialdom and suggested that we go to Stringfellows, the club to go to in London at that time. Ieuan Evans and Mike Hall were going to join us and get a taxi, but then Staff Jones, the miner from Ynysybwl, and a teammate of mine at Pontypool, said he wanted to come as well. I said, 'You three go on and I'll jump in a taxi with Staff and follow you there.' I wouldn't leave a teammate. When we arrived, there was a queue a mile long waiting to get in. As we were all still in dinner jackets, we went to the front of the queue and announced to the doormen, 'We're with the Jonathan Davies party.' Their response was, 'Come on in. There's a bucket of champagne waiting for you.' The week before, Jonathan had been on the *Wogan* show on the BBC and he must have organised something with Stringfellows in advance for this to be waiting. Once inside, we were shown the VIP area, but I was quite embarrassed as Webby nonchalantly lifted the red private rope and strode in.

I didn't really want to start drinking Jonathan's champagne. That feeling didn't last long – our entrance had attracted some very good-looking, smartly dressed girls who must have thought we were really important to be feted in this way. Mike Hall, who was a Cambridge University graduate, was quite good with the patter; Webby was outstanding. Ieuan and I didn't know what to do with ourselves and Staffers had disappeared! We cracked open the champagne, offered the girls a glass and were enjoying this taste of London high life. Just as we were relaxing, I noticed Staff several yards away at the bar. He shouted across the room, 'Boys! Boys! It's eight quid an effing half!' It certainly blew our cover and the girls just turned to us, looked down their noses and muttered, 'Riff Raff' before making a sharp exit! Ironically, Jonathan never showed up.

* * *

Although I consider myself very fortunate to have won thirty-two caps for Wales, I am still a bit saddened that injuries prevented me from having a longer playing career. I suppose injuries are part and parcel of what is, after all, a contact sport, but I was disappointed that a knee injury put me out of the game for eleven months after I'd just won four caps. At that time, I felt I'd had my best season ever, but the injury sustained against Swansea meant that I picked up the Player of the Year trophy in 1985 on crutches. The Young Player of the Year, by the way, was wing, Ieuan Evans.

Although when I resumed playing I might have lost a yard of pace, I adapted and gained another twenty-eight caps. It's not a bad record for club and country. Two hundred and fifty games for Cardiff, ninety-four tries and over six hundred and fifty points, including winning three Welsh Cup Finals and defeating a touring Grand Slam, Test-winning Australian side in 1984. I played for Wales in two World Cups – in 1987 (finishing third) and in 1991 – captained my country on two occasions when Wales toured Namibia in 1991 and I also represented the Barbarians.

Along with 'partner in crime' Glenn Webbe, I was

chosen to be part of Wales' World Cup squad for the inaugural tournament in 1987. The competition, co-hosted in Australia and New Zealand, proved very successful for us and we surprised everyone by finishing third, beating Australia along the way. When we first arrived for a tournament meeting with other players and representatives from all over the world, there was a big, shiny Mazda car on display in the middle of the hall where we all met. The organisers said that this car would be awarded to the scorer of the best try in the tournament, so you can imagine all the three quarters fancied their chances. The eventual winner was John Kirwan, the legendary All Blacks winger who seemed to beat all fifteen Italians on his way to scoring a remarkable try, one of the best I've ever seen.

My recollection of Wales' Mazda move is very different to Glenn's. We'd seen a move done by the French team, which was great, so we thought we'd try to copy it in one of the pool matches against Tonga. The outside half, Malcolm Dacey, would pass the ball to the inside centre, me, then I'd turn my back, Malcolm would loop around me, I would dummy him and then feint, to bring in the blindside winger. In this entire complicated manoeuvre, the ball would then actually be passed to the full back, Paul Thorburn, who was to come down the middle of the field.

The first part went OK, but Thorby came into the

line too soon, before Dacey got out of the way and he stood on his ankle. Malcolm never played again after that. The Tongans were formidable and very physical opponents, battering us at every opportunity. Glenn Webbe, who had already scored two tries, had been laid low by one particularly ferocious tackle and was out on his feet really. By then, we had used up our two replacements for Malcolm and Stuart Evans, but I was very concerned about my friend and told Richard Moriarty, the Welsh captain, 'Webby isn't right!'

Glenn came over to me and said, 'Where am I? I know you, but I don't know anyone else.' I'd never seen him cry in my life but there were tears rolling down his face. He was on the field playing for Wales, but, in reality, he was somewhere different. In the middle of this, I realised that my friend trusted me and that I was the only one he could really talk to. In a very tight match with the Tongans in full flow, we tried desperately to shield Glenn as much as possible. On one occasion though, instinct made me give the ball to him and mercifully he just ran down the middle, avoided the opposition, stopped at the post and just bent down slowly and dabbed the ball down like you do in sevens. I have never felt so relieved as I ran up to tell him what a brilliant try it was. It was one of three tries he scored that day but none of them merited the Mazda!

One great highlight of that tour was a grand pool

tournament organised by – you guessed it – Webby and me to relieve some of the monotony of staying in a not very nice hotel. It had very few facilities or amenities except for a pool table – with a slope. This was hardly conducive to tournament play but we had to make do. On top of that, in order to save money, we put beer mats in the pockets so that we could use the balls time and time again. The hotel must have lost a fortune. Everybody in the squad was made to play and the draw for the preliminary rounds matched me against Kevin Phillips, the Neath and Wales hooker.

By now, betting syndicates had been set up and I, the city boy, was odds on favourite to beat Kevin, the farmer from Cardigan. To everyone's surprise, I lost (I tried very hard to lose it), but to this day Kevin believes that he beat me fair and square. I made quite a bit of money on that match and, even though Kevin's odds came down considerably as a result of his first-round victory, he lost quite easily in the second round. This meant even more money for me, and Webby, although not knowing much about gambling, was very happy to invest, following my guidance. We eventually got to the final, billed as between Phil (Steve) Davies and Paul (Cliff) Thorburn. They were both pretty short odds, but by now our money was made.

The final would have done credit to the Crucible in Sheffield! Both players were dressed in dinner suits and dicky bows and Webby, as referee, also had the obligatory white gloves. In a match scheduled to be the best of five, Phil won on the very last black in the fifth game. Although for Webby and me it was a financially lucrative couple of days, I think the real value was the fact that the team came together in a common cause. Even the team management felt that this had been a great success and a worthwhile event.

* * *

After finishing playing, it seemed quite natural that I should turn to coaching. Strangely – though not surprisingly – in many ways, a lot of my methods are based on the old-school, simple, basic skills taught by PE teachers such as Mr Leek in St Albans School. As well as learning basic arithmetic in the classroom, I also learnt to count on the rugby field. This one element is, I think, the key to creative play: the ability to see where people are on the field, make quick decisions and thereby expose defences – all this because one teacher told me one day, 'Count! Look up and count.'

It seems to me nowadays that there is too much emphasis on structure and pre-planned moves. There seems little opportunity for playing and reacting to what is in front of you. Players seem frightened to take chances and to express themselves. Sadly, the result has been predictable, often boring rugby.

I absolutely love coaching because I'm striving to learn more every single day, and maybe bring something new to the game that's never been seen before. It's like the Holy Grail to me and is my main motivation. For me, coaching is all about the players, too many coaches think it's about them. I know I've had disagreements within clubs along the way, but I have to be true to myself. That's how I am and I can't help myself, there's nothing I can do about it.

As a youngster, growing up, I had my rugby heroes, the standouts being Barry John and Gerald Davies. I admired their pace, their quick thinking and their deft touches. Who have the present generation got to emulate? No one. They'd rather go home and play with their computers than sidestep lampposts in the way we used to on our way home. I remember Mike Rayer, the former Cardiff and Wales full back, telling me about this kid, Shane Williams, saying that he thought he was something special. How right he was! Despite being told he was too small, Shane stuck at it and became a box office draw international winger. When he did things on the rugby field, you sat up and took notice. There aren't enough players like that nowadays.

These days, I am still involved in coaching, but at a different level. My commitment is still the same and my motivation just as strong. I've never feared being given the sack – it's not nice because sometimes I can feel it coming, but I don't fear it. If I did, I would change my ways for the worse and I'd be negative.

My club these days is St Peters in Cardiff, an old

established team. I like to think that I treat them exactly as I would a first class club; I respect their players and pass on to them tried and tested methods of playing this great game. As well as this, I do feel a sense of responsibility for the next generation of rugby players. What legacy can I leave them? My contribution these days is arranging a number of affordable rugby camps where children of all abilities can come together, learn and, most importantly, enjoy the game. They learn the skills of the game, but they also make great friends and learn life skills, as I did. I owe that to my teachers and to my family.

CHAPTER SEVEN

Introduction by Richard Moriarty
Swansea RFC, Wales

First and foremost, Glenn Webbe was an extremely good rugby player and thoroughly deserving of his place in the Welsh team. As captain of the side that finished third in the 1987 inaugural World Cup, I was very fortunate in having a three-quarter line which consisted of great players like Robert Jones, Jonathan Davies, John Devereux and Adrian Hadley to name a few. Glenn Webbe on the wing was of equal standard to them.

A superb athlete, he posed a real attacking threat. If you gave him space, gave him the ball, then the opposition defence would be sorely tested. Often, those trying to tackle him were made to look very foolish, as Glenn scored yet another try.

Although I was extremely proud to be the captain of that World Cup team, my role was made much easier because of the quality of the players, both on and off the field. Glenn was the consummate tourist, confident, likeable, talented and always up for a bit of 'light entertainment'. He had tricks up his sleeve for every occasion, just the thing to keep spirits up when you're a long way from home and facing tough rugby international matches on a regular basis. In turn, Glenn appreciated, more than most, the importance of the team as a whole and the effort that his fellow players had put in so that he could score the tries. He was a superb finisher, though modest in his success. A outstanding physical specimen in terms of fitness, Glenn would not be out of place in the modern game.

Did he have any other qualities? Yes, his singing was excellent. I think he was the forerunner of karaoke and never passed up an opportunity to burst into song to the delight of teammates and other audiences alike. Almost thirty years on from that World Cup, I am delighted to sing Glenn's praises – he is one of the really great characters of rugby football.

Glenn Webbe

Bridgend RFC, Barbarians, Wales

I always loved rugby, from a very early age. I played for my school, Glan Ely High School in Cardiff, from the age of eleven. We weren't a great team, and we used to lose far more games than we won, but we tried our best! Our games teachers, Mr Bartley, Mr Smart and Mr Winterburn, were hugely important in giving their time to us. My school reports showed clearly that, in academic subjects, 'Glenn could do more', but in PE and Games it was always A+. I started playing rugby at outside half, then I was put into the centre, then full back and eventually ended up on the wing. Why? Simple. I didn't pass the ball … I just ran as fast as I could!

When I was older, a friend of mine, Dennis Paine, asked me to join Canton RFC – his brother Chrissie was playing for the youth team at that time. The only other option was Glamorgan Wanderers, but they were a first class team then and being just kids, we wouldn't have had a look in. Canton Youth, however, had lots of players who were moving up to senior level and therefore had several team places to fill.

I joined the club and, with all my teammates, used to go down on the number fourteen bus from Ely, getting off by Market Road, where the police station used to be, to walk across to Llandaff Fields. Canton RFC didn't have a clubhouse so we all congregated in The Butchers Arms.

It was a very busy time for me as a young, enthusiastic player. I started playing two games of rugby in one day: I played for the school team in the morning with a 10 a.m. kick-off and then I'd run straight down to Llandaff Fields for a 3 p.m. kick-off to play for Canton RFC as a youth player in the afternoon. I was in the youth team for three years and loved my time playing there alongside my mates from school, Dennis Paine, Howard Martin and Billy Nicholls. We never got tired and just thoroughly enjoyed ourselves going from game to game. We weren't a particularly strong side, but we more than made up for that with team spirit and support for each other. It has always been the camaraderie, the friendships and the fun that have kept me in the game; the togetherness has always been really important to me.

During this time, Caerau started a youth team and made an approach for all us Ely boys to play for them as we all lived in the area. By then, we had established ourselves in Canton; we were just together and we stayed together. You can imagine when Canton Youth then got to play Caerau Youth! It was a very hard game and I think that they were trying to cause as much damage as possible to the Ely boys who had gone astray. I can honestly say that I got most of my speed from those games – it was the fear of getting caught!

It was a really happy time; all we wanted to do was just play rugby. As well as the approach from Caerau, some rugby league scouts came down to look at players and I even had a couple of meetings with Widnes. Bobby Farnham, the youth coach then, fended off all these lucrative offers and, as a result, I stayed with Canton. Bobby is still, to this day, a very good friend.

The next logical step was to play for the Cardiff and District youth side. The step up was quite marked. It was a bit like the first taste of representative honours and I was very proud to be part of the team. It was nice to think that the selectors for that team had seen me play for Canton and thought I was good enough to join the squad, in which the majority of players played for Cardiff Youth. There were a lot of successful players like Mike Budd, Adrian Hadley and myself from smaller clubs like Canton and St Josephs. The coaches warned us that we weren't likely to get a Welsh Youth cap from our smaller clubs and told us that we should join Cardiff if we wanted to go forward.

We had a discussion in The Dusty Forge pub in Ely after a district game and we felt we should be selected on whether we were good enough, not where we came from. We all agreed and made a pact that we would not go to play for Cardiff, but that we would stay with our clubs. If we didn't get a Welsh cap coming from our teams, representing the people we really were, then we wouldn't deserve one anyway. We all stayed in those teams on principle and I got capped from Canton and Adrian and Mike were capped from St Josephs. We enjoyed each other's company and we stuck by our guns and, looking back, I do feel proud we stood firm and I'm glad we did it.

I had two seasons as a Welsh Youth player because of my age group. In the second year, I remember playing against England at Oxford. We lost that game, but I had a good friend, Andrew Phillips, who was also coming to the end of his time as a youth player. I was anxious that Andrew should have some game time, but tactical substitutions were not allowed then. Anyway, about fifteen minutes before the end of the game, I fell, pole-axed, to the ground, claiming that I had been given a dead leg by one of our English opponents. It wasn't as bad as my acting, but nevertheless I limped off and Andrew got to play for Wales Youth in his last season.

* * *

GLENN WEBBE

My dad, Hugh Michael Athill, was a foundry worker in Cardiff. He kept himself fit all his working life. He had played football while serving in the army and walked every day to work, even in his last job at the age of eighty-two. Everybody liked my dad. He was a happy-go-lucky man with a very strong work ethic and I like to think I inherited those traits from him.

At home, I was the only boy ... with seven sisters: Bernadette, Paulette, Humie, Sondra, Jacqueline, Avril and Veronica. I made up for that by having the most impressive-sounding name: Glenfield Michael Charles Webbe. The Glenfield is an old West Indian name, which came from my mum, Islyn's, side of the family. There wasn't a lot of rugby influence from the girls, but my family supported me through everything and my dad came to most of my games. He didn't really know a lot about rugby, as he was a football man: he had played for Arsenal St Kitts from the age of thirteen and he had been the youngest player in the team. Nothing stopped him being there for me.

I always remember going to one game in Moseley in my first season. We had to get there early and it was an overnight stay. As we came down to the pitch, one of the boys piped up, 'There's a man down by the posts who doesn't half look like your dad!' I looked and it was him! He had come on his own by train, as he didn't drive, but was determined to travel all that way to see me. It was an effort, especially after working long hours, but he had got himself there to support me. He came on the coach with the boys back to where we were staying, then he hopped on a train to go back home again. He was never one to push me, but I shall never forget those selfless acts of fatherly love.

When I was in school, many of my friends couldn't understand what my dad was saying when he talked to them. He had a deep West Indian accent and also a stammer. He realised that people couldn't work out what he was saying so he would repeat things several times to try to make himself clear. When my school friends called they asked if he was speaking a West Indian language and looked to me to help them understand what he had said to them. I pretended that I spoke it too, 'translating' for them and enjoying their amazed looks. It was only years later I told them the truth!

I was selected to tour South Africa with the Wales Youth side, winning my cap from Canton. Looking back, I like to think that I was selected on merit from my small club. I was quick, had self-belief, a great desire to do my very best and was determined not to let my country down. Politically, it was a difficult time to be going to South Africa. The British Lions who were out there playing had already faced criticism for supporting the apartheid regime, but for a young sportsman like me, it was important to see for myself what was going on while enjoying the friendship and camaraderie of teammates. I didn't know at the time, but my dad was also subjected to criticism from friends who were not happy that I was touring. I had no idea what to expect, as at home I had lived very happily in a multicultural city. In South Africa, though, my eyes were opened to the reality of the situation. I'm glad that I went there to see what was going on at first hand.

I did experience racism there myself, on one occasion when we were all invited to a restaurant for dinner. We were some of the first to get there and be seated, but we began to notice that tables of diners arriving after us were instantly attended to. One of the lads, who was known for being quite blunt, pointed out that it was because of me that we were not being served. I laughed, but the restaurant then informed us that they didn't serve black people. It was the first time that I had really been faced with anything like that and I couldn't believe it was happening.

A few nights later, we were invited back to the same place in an official capacity as part of the Welsh touring party. I was there with my Welsh blazer on and this time, they seemed happy to serve us. The speeches were full of glowing praise for the tour, but I felt I had to say that they had been unable and unwilling to serve me a few days earlier. This got back to Henry Hurley, the Chairman of Cardiff and District Rugby Union and member of the management team, who spoke up on my behalf. They offered to change their rules this time, but it was too late and I'm proud to say we all got up and left without eating. It was a very positive thing for him to have done for me and I admired him for that loyalty. The tour was a wonderful bonding experience. It taught us a great deal about the power of sticking together and supporting each other as a team, and also as human beings.

I came straight from youth rugby to play for Bridgend, my one and only first class club. My original intention was to go there for a couple of seasons and then, quite naturally, as a Cardiff boy, to go back and play for my home town club if things went well. I was encouraged to join Bridgend by my good mate Robbie James and, as things turned out, on my debut I scored four tries against Mid Glamorgan County. In the second game, I scored three tries against Cross Keys – it was the best start!

The people at the club were so welcoming and made me feel very much part of a new team. It was captained in my first year by prop Meredydd James, an exceptional leader, who many felt was very unlucky not to have won an international cap. Unfortunately for him, the sitting tenant was Graham Price, one of the famous Pontypool front row.

In that first year, we beat Cardiff home and away and I scored a total of five tries in those two games. I thought then, 'I'm better off here' and I stopped feeling that I needed to fulfil a dream of playing for Cardiff.

GLENN WEBBE

Bridgend was a very honest place and I liked the fact people there genuinely wanted to get to know me and accepted me for who I was. I enjoyed playing with good players, and the backs, particularly, were full of invention and flair, creating plenty of space for me as the wing to run the tries in.

In one re-arranged game against Blackwood in the Welsh Cup, I scored six tries before getting a twinge in my hamstring. The match was in some doubt due to adverse weather conditions and, as was the practice in those days, the ground had been covered in straw. Up to the time of my injury in that game, things had gone really well and some of the papers began to refer to me as, 'Webbe the wonder wing, the one to watch'.

Everything about Bridgend seemed so right. The club had a structure and a code of conduct, which we players signed up to. On match days, we wore club blazers, collar and tie and always ate together before the game. We would then, as a squad, meet up and everyone had to contribute and talk about their individual performance. Waiting for your turn to speak was christened 'the creeping death', but we had to do it and it was good for team morale. I owe a lot to the Bridgend club and still keep in touch with teammates. Nowadays, they have a big reunion for former players and I really look forward to that as a way of catching up with old friends and recounting old matches and stories.

RUGBY GENERATIONS

One of the great characters at Bridgend and a good friend of mine was Martin Daly. Every time someone asked him, 'How do you spell that?' he said, 'Daly ... no e, no I, just ly!' We shared the same sense of humour and a certain ongoing incident could be the original soap opera! It started in the showers, in the Brewery Field changing rooms after a game. Martin didn't have any soap so I offered him mine. At first, he said he wouldn't bother, but then very reluctantly took it, showered and handed it back. Later on, as we sat down to a meal together after the game, he went to his pocket and miraculously found the bit of soap, which I had carefully dried off and placed there. At the end of the evening, as I went home, he got his own back, as by now, the soap had been returned into my jacket pocket. This went on for about a year, the by now tiny, much-travelled bar of soap to-ing and fro-ing between us and finding its way into kit bags, various items of clothing and even served up with a flourish on a silver salver at a restaurant we were both in. I had to have the last word though, so one day, as the final act in this story, I put the sliver of soap in an envelope and posted it to Martin's family home. I can still vividly remember writing 'Martin Daly, 57 Princes Street, Roath, Cardiff'. Very silly, I know, but good – clean – fun!

We regularly played against Maesteg RFC, a nearby club and always a difficult game. These were tough matches and both teams were desperate to beat each other. They would do anything to try to disrupt us and they succeeded with me; it was the first time that I had been sent off in my life. Sin binning had been brought in and I was to learn about it the hard way. In the quarter final of the Schweppes Cup, I scored a try, popped the ball down and, as I was jogging back, one of the Maesteg forwards elbowed me in the face. I hit the deck, sprang up and attacked him, and this ended up in a mass brawl between the two teams. The referee broke it up and approached me with a stern face. I was so concerned that a red card would mean I couldn't play in the Cup Final, all I could do was repeat to myself, 'Don't send me off. Don't send me off.' Thankfully, he didn't bring the red card out of his pocket but showed me the yellow card – the first for Bridgend!

Again, in another game at Maesteg, the crowd were determined to rile us and put us off. I was adamant that I wouldn't react, as to do so would mean they had won; they would have achieved what they wanted to. So I tried to dismiss all of the cat-calling and names. However, I could hear in the distance, 'Webbe, Webbe', getting louder and louder and then I heard 'Glenno', so I thought then it might be someone who knew me. I turned around to look and, as I did so, a banana came flying at me from the crowd, landing right between my feet. This was very different, not the usual crowd banter. I stared at it, picked it up slowly, unpeeled it, took a bite and threw it back into the direction of the person it came from. I carried on playing and hoped I had defused the situation with humour rather than reacting in the way that the individual who had thrown it had clearly hoped for.

The world is a different place now, thankfully. Today, it wouldn't be tolerated and the person concerned would be ejected from the crowd and banned. I tried to put myself into understanding the thought process of that person. Imagine the effort wasted in going to buy a banana, waiting to throw it at me and thinking he had won by such awful behaviour, instead of just enjoying the game and getting the most out of his day. I took it as a compliment that I couldn't be that bad a player if people felt the need to try and hurt or upset me in this way. Why else would you waste all that negative energy?

My dad never outwardly worried about me at a rugby game, though I'm sure he was concerned about that kind of treatment. Every time he came to a match, the team and supporters treated him very well and he loved it. He was, however, worried when I was approached to go on a rebel tour to play in South Africa. A lot of money was offered around that time to entice people to go, but I listened to him and could sense his real concern. It was a lot of money to turn down at the time – others were able to buy houses with their tour fees – but my dad's worries were far too important to me and I didn't take up any offer. Years previously, I had wanted to go on the Wales Youth tour of South Africa to find out for myself what was going on there. Having seen and experienced with my own eyes the nature of apartheid, it reinforced my decision not to visit that country again until the political system was changed, lucrative though it may have been at the time.

Dad was incredibly proud when I made my debut for Wales v Tonga in 1986 in Nuku'alofa. To be selected to play for Wales represented my life's ambition. I had thought that I would be pulling on the red jersey, but my debut for Wales was in green! I didn't care what colour jersey I played in, I was now a Welsh international and I became the first black player to represent my country at rugby union. To be part of the World Cup squad in 1987 was equally thrilling. I had never experienced anything like it in my whole life. The management team consisted of manager Clive Rowlands and coaches, Derek Quinnell and Tony Gray, but in the training sessions back home before leaving we had a secret weapon. In a series of special fitness sessions aimed at getting us properly prepared we were led by Olympic gold medallist 'Lynn the Leap' Davies. It was quite an eye opener. At the World Cup were sixteen teams of the best players all in one competition, and I was just in awe of the faces lined up there who were all heroes to me. John Kirwan, the great All Black wing, who I had watched and admired for so long, actually knew my name: 'Hello Webbe. Bridgend,' he said when we first met. He actually knew I existed – I was amazed! On reflection, the great man had obviously done his homework and knew all the players in the wing position. Still a great moment though!

We were shown a gleaming car that had been taken on to the pitch, a Mazda, which was to be the prize for the scorer of the best try in the tournament. At the end of each day, there would be a list of contenders for this great prize. Mark Ring, a superb maverick teammate, would come up with great ideas of how we could win this. He was a creative, talented player who couldn't understand why others were unable to see the possibilities he could for scoring fantastic tries that he was certainly capable of pulling off. He was determined to win that Mazda car! He came up with all sorts of outstanding moves to get on to the list for try of the day, in order to work towards the ultimate prize he wanted.

We finally came up with a series of moves he named … 'Mazda'. It never worked in training, as we kept reminding him, but he was still sure it could. In the match against Tonga, a bruising forward battle, we managed to hold our own in the scrums. However, we were absolutely battered by the Tongans in the loose that day, with prop Stuart Evans and outside half

GLENN WEBBE

Malcolm Dacey forced to leave the pitch after we tried to execute the Mazda move. I was fortunate enough to have scored two tries in the game, but neither of them would have been good enough to win the car. Later in the game, I was laid low with a crunching tackle; I was smacked hard and lay, completely out of it, on the floor. Eventually, I came around, but couldn't leave the pitch as we had used up all our replacements because of earlier injuries.

The Tongans kept coming at us with wave after wave of huge attacks. When one of those broke down, Mark Ring, instead of kicking the ball safely into touch, passed the ball to me and, still not fully recovered and on automatic pilot, I ran quite some distance and scored my third try of the game. This was the try that was entered into the Mazda competition! Sadly, the great John Kirwan's try against Italy won and the Mazda was never ours. We won the game, but lost the car! Even worse, because of the protocol of the day, Clive Rowlands, the manager, came to tell me that I had to be sent home due to having had concussion. I pleaded, telling him I was fine, but he insisted that it was for my own good. Stuart Evans was sent home too with a broken ankle and the final straw for me was that I had to carry his bags as he was injured! I was devastated to leave the team and the tour at such an important time.

Looking back, I can't help thinking that much of the

fun and enjoyment I had playing rugby was due in no small part to my great friend, fellow prankster and mischief maker Mark Ring. We go back a long way together and on tour, particularly, we were inseparable. If, as did happen, Mark was down to room with somebody other than myself, I'd make sure that I evicted that person pretty sharpish! On one occasion, Cardiff and Wales centre Mike Hall incurred my 'wrath'. Having been told he was to share with Ringy, he arrived at the room, unpacked and hung up all his clothes in the most beautifully ordered way – everything had its place. He was not best pleased when I knocked on the door and said, 'Out you go! I'm in here,' but fair play to Mike, he took the hint and left.

Touring, for me, was the icing on the cake, and being part of the World Cup squad in 1987 was fantastic. The hard part was getting picked, but having been given my opportunity, I was going to make the most of it. I was as fit as I had ever been, never tired, and worked very hard in training. I was determined to enjoy myself, however, and I couldn't resist the odd practical joke even on a tour as important as this.

As always, I had visited a couple of joke shops and armed myself with a few little novelty props that I thought would come in useful at some stage. On this occasion, I carried a little toy – a cap banger – wherever I went. I would set it down when people were having a drink and, as they raised their glass, bang, off went the toy and the drink was spilt all over the place. I loved it! At night, just before Ringy went to sleep, he had a habit of turning his pillow over – just the place to put the banger. One night he came in and, being a creature of habit adjusted the pillow, said, 'Goodnight Webby,' and as he put his head down to sleep – bang! He was not best pleased …

He did get his revenge though, in a roundabout way. Mark had brought with him the very latest aftershave, which he loved, called Paco Rabanne. I used to dab it on without his knowing, but Ringy, ever suspicious, would accuse me of using it without his permission. I denied this vigorously and even feigned shock that my friend could accuse me of such a thing. He then marked the bottle to try to catch me out, but again, without him knowing, I carefully rubbed out the mark and put a new line on the bottle. Anyway, one morning, before going to training, I rummaged around in my kit bag for my toy banger, but there was no sign of it anywhere. I searched the room frantically for it, but it had disappeared. I went late to training in a bad mood and lunchtime, normally the time I would set the banger off, passed without incident. It was the worst lunch I'd ever had! Mark told me not to worry about it, but I was really upset.

Later that night, after more training, I said, 'I'm going up to have a shower. I'll catch up with you later'. After my shower and, having changed into fresh clothes, I thought 'He's not here. I'll just use some of his Paco Rabanne.' I picked up the bottle and – bang! There was my toy. Mark had caught me at it. There was no way now that I could say I hadn't been using his precious aftershave. He found me out good and proper and got his revenge. That's exactly how Mark operates – he works you out, bides his time and then catches you out!

Although it might seem that all our rugby-playing days together were one big laugh, we did take the game seriously. Mark Ring, I think, was a player of outstanding talent, you never quite knew what he was going to do next and certainly the opposition didn't! He was a natural player and never fully realised how much talent he had. He is also an extremely gifted coach and likes nothing better than passing on his great knowledge of the game to young players.

Singing was also an integral part of touring in those days. I love to sing and my sisters do too. Jackie went on to win *Stars in their Eyes*, the *X Factor* of its day. Music and singing was always part of the Webbe household. Even in Wales Youth days, while travelling by coach to different venues, I would lead the boys from East Wales in song, while Robbie James from Carmarthen, who had a lovely voice, tried to prove that the boys from the west were best. In the end, we had little competitions between our groups and, as a sort of finale, would all join together in harmony. We used to sing a lot of anthems and put our own slant on some of the old Welsh hymn favourites.

Singing was also a major factor in our World Cup exploits in 1987. When we beat England in the quarter final, in the presentation after the game, Paul Moriarty serenaded our departing opponents with *I'm leaving on a jet plane,* just to rub it in. Tour manager, Clive Rowlands, who loved – and still loves – choral singing urged me, and all my Welsh teammates, to sing on every possible occasion. The team that sings together plays together.

Although I never really followed rugby, as such, as a youngster, preferring to play rather than watch, I have to say that one of my heroes was Gerald Davies. On one occasion, on a Sports Council for Wales youth-rugby week in Aberystwyth, I met up with my hero and thoroughly enjoyed talking to him. The following season, I was a steward at one of the international matches, showing people to their seats. Along came Gerald and asked, 'Where am I sitting, Webby?' He'd remembered me from the year before and I was really proud of that. To think that I went on to play on the wing for Wales just like Gerald did makes that meeting so very special.

I am lucky to have been successful in a sport that I love. I was utterly dedicated to rugby and wanted to do as well as I could for the team I was playing for. I am happy with what I have achieved. I have been called a pioneer, but I believe it is in all of us to do well. Seizing the opportunity is what matters. Luck plays a big part, but determination and hard work bring success. Rugby is special in the way that it brings people together. Players of all sizes, genders and backgrounds come together for the love of the game. Everyone has something to offer a team; there are leaders, doers and followers and they can all play a part for the common good of that team.

My parents were always proud of us all. My sisters are all achievers and have done well in their chosen fields. Now, my wife Sally and I are the proud parents of two daughters, Lily and Marcy. I will be there for them whatever they decide to do, just as my parents were there for me. They never pushed me, but were always there with love and total support. I would like to be the same for my daughters.

CHAPTER EIGHT

Introduction by Byron Hayward
Ebbw Vale RFC, Llanelli RFC, Gloucester, Wales

I'm pleased to say that Kingsley's mother and my mother are now very good friends. It wasn't always so, because years back they had the most almighty row, as a result of a huge fight between him and me. We were five years old at the time … yes, we go back a long way!

The reason for that initial clash was that we were, and still are, very competitive and it was that competitiveness that forged a firm friendship, which has lasted to this day.

As kids, when we chose rugby sides to play one another, Kingsley was very shrewd, always grabbing first pick, so ensuring that he would get the best players. We played together for Nantyglo under-11s mini rugby side and got our first taste of playing on the famous Cardiff Arms Park even then. We were entered into a national competition and although no one gave us a chance, as we were up against some big guns in mini rugby terms, the rank outsiders won! Nantyglo, with Kingsley and me in the team, were crowned champions, much to the delight of our travelling supporters who included my much-loved grandfather, one of the few occasions he saw me play before his passing.

Little did we know then that, one day, the two boys from the council estate in Blaina would play rugby for Wales and, like every team we were in since the under-11s, we would play our hearts out for one another and for our teammates. There was a huge bond and togetherness between us.

As a player, Kingsley had the heart of a lion. Not the biggest physically, he gave everything on the field and I can bear painful testimony to the fact that he was an extremely hard tackler. He could also take the bumps himself and keep going and going. He was a natural leader, captaining virtually every team he played for; he led from the front and didn't wait for anyone else to do the hard work.

Kingsley loved to wind up the opposition and was quick to enjoy some banter with referees as well. A real character who had a rapport with players and supporters alike, his deep knowledge of the game served him well as a player, and now makes him a first class coach.

INTRODUCTION: BYRON HAYWARD

We grew up together, played rugby together, and have shared both good and bad times. He is somebody who will always tell you the truth. He is totally honest and his heart is in the right place. Kingsley Jones is one of the best friends I've ever had.

Kingsley Jones

Ebbw Vale RFC, Gloucester, Worcester,
Pontypridd RFC, Barbarians, Wales

Rugby has always been a major part of my life. My earliest memory is playing for Nantyglo mini rugby team at the age of five. I remember running around and receiving a trophy in 1975 with 'Pontllanfraith Winner' engraved on the bottom. Coming from Blaina, I had great role models who played for Wales like Mike Ruddock, the former Wales coach, outside half, Dai Watkins and lock, Bob Norster. The rugby club was the centre of everything in our coal-mining village. I grew up chasing the ball on Central Park in Blaina while watching my dad, also named Kingsley Jones, play. Dad was captain of Blaina in their centenary season in 1975. He also played a few seasons at Ebbw Vale and we would walk over the mountain to support him. It was a big thing for me, as a kid, to go to Eugene Cross Park, a very big stadium as it seemed to me then!

Growing up, I think my kit was comprised of one

pair of shorts and one rugby jersey. The local tip was our playground and I remember that I had an old leather ball that had split at the seams. The only thing left was the bladder inside but, undeterred, we just got on with playing with that. Later, I was given a Leeds United and a Newport County football top, but I never got to own a replica rugby kit like the ones so many young children have today. I lived four doors away from Byron Hayward and I think it is quite remarkable that two close neighbours and friends ended up playing for Wales and that, later, both of us pursued a career in rugby coaching.

Despite being great friends, we were extremely competitive and we would have a fight at least once a week. It was a bit like sibling rivalry really, but winning was everything. The rugby matches on the tip were planned with care and precision. Byron and I were the respective selectors, managers and captains of the opposing teams and ended up telling our team members exactly what to do. The two of us had played mini rugby in Nantyglo from a very young age, so we saw ourselves as the experts on tactics and the laws of the game.

From the tips, we graduated to a patch of grass outside my friend Russell Ball's home but, despite the change of venue, it was still the same old faces who assembled to play hard-fought rugby and soccer matches and games of British Bulldog! In my mind's eye, I was Terry Cobner, or Bobby Windsor from Pontypool, or Clive Burgess from Ebbw Vale – all great international players. As my dad was a prop, I saw myself either as a front row or a back row forward, a 'go and get the ball' type of player. Lots of my friends pretended to be Phil Bennett or JJ Williams, but I didn't see myself in those positions. Byron Hayward imagined he was the next Barry John; there couldn't have been more of a contrast between two such close friends. Unusually for a prop forward, Dad also kicked penalties and conversions for Blaina and I, too, fancied myself as a goal kicker, as well as a hard-working forward.

When I was ten, and playing for Nantyglo, we won a preliminary competition which meant we were through to play in the final at Cardiff Arms Park, the National Stadium. Nantyglo won the South Wales Echo tournament and out of that victorious, very young team, Byron Hayward and I were fortunate enough to go on to play rugby for Wales in later years.

We were undefeated for a couple of years in that age group. They were great times and my father was always there to watch me. He always talked to me about the importance of the team. Another thing he kept stressing to me was to get the ball, not just to wait for the ball. I knew how important that was to him. The advice he gave me repeatedly when I played, was to go and get involved. He said, 'If you wait for the ball, the game will pass you by.' That was probably why I ended up playing as a hooker or a flanker.

I was fortunate enough to be in both the school rugby team and football team in Nantyglo Comprehensive School. I was a central midfielder in soccer, and ran about a lot, a bit like my rugby playing, always trying to get the ball. Rugby, though, was the dominant game as we only played soccer about five times a year. I don't remember us ever having a school cricket team. We only played it as part of PE. Although this was normal to me at the time, I realised as I got older how limited our sports choices were compared with today. We had regular rugby matches against schools like Rose Hayworth, Six Bells and Brynmawr, but little else. Nowadays, there are so many sporting options for young people to try, but then there was much less choice. Our gymnasium was like a Portakabin, with basic apparatus, unlike today's gyms full of the latest physical training equipment.

Phil Bowker was my PE teacher and he was excellent. He understood me and he knew how to manage me. I was always the 'chopsy', cheeky one. We used to have a bin of daps in the corner of the gym, and if you spoke too much or misbehaved, you had to pick a dap from the bin and suffer the consequences! I used to end up having the dap nearly every lesson and it became a big joke to everyone. Privately, I used to call him Batman Bowker, it was a secret nickname, but he knew I called him that. He obviously had a good sense of humour, as one day I was given the dap, even though I hadn't done anything. On the bottom of the dap, he had written in big letters 'POW!' ... Batman Bowker strikes again! I saw him about fifteen years ago and recognised him immediately. Looking back, although he was essentially a soccer man, he knew his rugby and was a big influence on me.

When I was about twelve, my mother and father divorced and my father emigrated to New Zealand. He wrote to me regularly and, from his letters, I learnt he was playing rugby in New Zealand and had started coaching at Grammar rugby club in Auckland. Their squad included twin brothers Alan and Gary Whetton, the great All Blacks, a Fijian international wing, Jimi Damu, and the Canadian number eight, Glen Ennis.

I can't pretend that the next few formative years were easy, because I missed my dad, however, I just got on with it like most boys do at that age. I went out playing with my mates, went camping and continued my rugby. It was too expensive then to make phone calls – there was no Skype or FaceTime in those days – and airmail letters were the main form of communication. But although he wrote to me, I was not the best at replying.

* * *

When I was eighteen, I went over to New Zealand and started playing there. My father was coaching all these great players I'd only read about in his letters and now these men became huge influences on me and my playing career. I went with my dad to all sorts of amazing coaching seminars and had the privilege of listening to and watching players of the calibre of lock Andy Haden and the All Blacks kicking machine, Grant Fox. All of these wonderful experiences were made possible because my dad was involved in coaching within the New Zealand rugby union. In those two years I progressed and learnt so much as a player and as a person. I couldn't believe that I was fortunate enough to be able to do all this. The highlight for me was when the fantastic All Blacks flanker, Alan Whetton, came around to the house to have tea with us. Could it get any better?

It's difficult to explain what makes New Zealand so great at rugby, but I think it's partly cultural. Many of the people are mentally and physically tough, many of them come from farming stock: they just get on with it, a mentality that's suited to rugby. They have a lot of pride and an amazing ability to overcome adversity and never give up whatever the odds. I think too, as in Wales, that because rugby has played such an important part in the development of communities, it has become an integral part of life. Everything revolves around the game – playing, supporting or socialising. Maori and Polynesian influences have also been a huge factor in making New Zealand the world champions that they are.

Although there were many similarities between the rugby circles I was used to at home and my new-found experiences in New Zealand, the main difference I discovered was that the New Zealand players seemed to take the games more seriously. They seemed more driven, more competitive and single-minded, attitudes shared by their close neighbours in Australia. Even at the lowest level of rugby, there was a determination to succeed. Training sessions were taken seriously and woe betide anyone who failed to turn up or was late. Retribution from coaches was quick and ruthless. Very simply, if you didn't turn up for training, you didn't get picked.

For a small population, they also had a remarkable strength in depth. As an incomer trying to make his mark, I was always looking over my shoulder, as I knew there would be a very good New Zealander champing at the bit to take my place. I also became very aware of the need to eat properly. Eating habits and nutrition are very much part of the New Zealand rugby players' fitness regime. As a valleys boy, I had grown up on fish fingers, chips and beans, now I had to embrace salads and vegetables! Fitness, in New Zealand terms, was on a different level to anything I was used to. I remember somebody saying a fit player makes an average player good, a good player very good and a very good player an international. I never forgot that, and worked extremely hard to be as good as they were. It was a complete change of lifestyle for me, and a change that was well worth it.

* * *

My first game in New Zealand was as part of a Sevens team from Ardmore in Counties, the region next door to Auckland and the region that developed All Black legend, Jonah Lomu. We played at Pukekohe stadium and our team progressed well. It included a number of great players such as John Bell, who played for Counties no end of times, the Marsh brothers (Tony Marsh later went on to play for France), Junior Paramore, the Samoan international, and Vern Cotter, the former coach of Scotland. He was straight down the line, tough and resilient and a huge influence on my mental approach to the game.

I was very proud to be part of that team and it was great to rub shoulders with such excellent players. As I progressed within the club, I was either chosen to play or be on the bench – quite an achievement for a young kid from overseas. I was fortunate that I could cover as a hooker or flanker for them, invaluable, as you were only allowed two replacements in those days. It was a huge learning curve and I realised that I needed to be at the top of my game at all times. If you weren't, you didn't last long. Literally, it was the survival of the fittest.

Ardmore seemed a long way from Blaina and the

valley clubs, where a promising rugby player would be welcomed into the club with a 'Come on in, butt! Have a cup of tea, some chips and if you want to play for us, we'll pick you next week.' That didn't happen in New Zealand, in fact no one really spoke to me at first. The turning point, I think, came at a trial match where I handed off Robert Kururangi, a former All Black, who ended up on the floor. From then on, I gained some respect and certainly more friends within the club. I had proven myself. I was now accepted as one of them.

* * *

Returning to Wales, still as a very young man, was a huge culture shock. I had spent two years being around legendary New Zealand players who had just won the first ever World Cup. Their drive and determination encouraged me to try to pursue my long-time ambition to play senior rugby. I played with Brynmawr Youth, and then was lucky enough to be invited to join Abertillery, who were a top side at the time.

I was one of the fittest players in pre-season training and, luckily for me, Peter Crane, who had been a great servant of Abertillery, left the club, which led to a vacancy in the back row. I had a trial for them and they offered me fifteen starts and a trip to Florida in May of that year. That was how it was then, you signed for the teams that had the best tour! Abertillery were going for one week to Fort Lauderdale and one week to Disney World so I thought, 'Let's do it!' I did play fifteen games; I would have liked to have played more, but I broke my wrist in October. The club stuck to their guns and, as promised, I went with them to Fort Lauderdale and Orlando. Although I wasn't able to play, I still kept up my training – in New Zealand, I had started going to the gym for the first time – nice weather also made a difference; there were no real excuses for missing sessions.

Back home, things were quite different. I had transferred to Ebbw Vale, where Nigel Meek, also from Blaina, was a big influence. There was a gym in Nantyglo leisure centre with little weights, but there was nothing like the gym I had been used to. I did try and keep as fit as I could though by cycling from home to training sessions. The wet Welsh winters didn't help, and I felt myself slipping back into bad habits. I wasn't as fit as I had been in New Zealand. The biggest change, however, was the very different lifestyle. In New Zealand after a match you would just have a beer, some food and go home, as the clubhouse would be closed at 9 p.m. In Wales, it was customary to stay in the clubhouse all night and see how many pints you could drink. I was hopeless! No wonder players were struggling on the Sunday and for training during the rest of the week.

On the morning of a game, I would eat half a chicken and some lettuce, I don't know why, as it contained protein but no carbohydrate at all. The advice nowadays would be very different. I should have been eating chicken and protein after the match, not before! In those days, there weren't any nutritionists and physios with you all the time, so you didn't know any different. On match days, as in training, I would always be the first at the ground, even before the coach – I was just keen really. Timing has always been important to me.

I had a number of jobs at this time. A friend of my dad's had a wine bar in Ebbw Vale and I got a job working behind the bar. I ended up running the place, but it wasn't good for my rugby. We had training on a Monday night but there was karaoke in the bar that evening too, so I ended up having to go there afterwards to supervise things. The smoke in the place was incredible and, although working in the evenings gave me plenty of time off to go running, swimming and cycling, I did think that maybe manual labour would be better to keep up my fitness levels.

I made the decision to go and work with Terry Williams, a local builder. I knew him well and I really enjoyed my time working with him. My week now had a structure to it: I would work hard Monday, Tuesday, Wednesday and then ease off towards the end of the week ready for the game. I would do the minimum then, make the tea and make any excuse to go to the builder's yard. He jokes now that if he wanted anything done it always had to be at the beginning of the week! He would ask me to move five tons of sand and I would set myself a target to move it in an hour. I'd be covered in sweat as a result of my exertions, so then I'd have lunch and rest, happy that I had reached my goal and was keeping fit in the process. I still enjoy manual labour. I'd be just as happy if I could earn good money on the shovel.

I became a father when I was very young. With fatherhood came responsibility, which in turn, helped my self-discipline and my rugby-playing career. I had two boys, Rhys and Dorian. They had the same upbringing as me – rugby non-stop. I used to call Dorian my shadow. He loved watching games on television, knew most of the players by name, and often joined in the commentary. He even prepared for those matches by taping his wrists and wearing headgear. Rugby was all!

Getting picked to play for Wales is a huge honour and I still have all the letters from the WRU in a bag at home. It was a big thrill to receive the special stationery with the three feathers embossed on it, telling me I had been selected. It was a dream come true. Very recently, I received a letter from WRU Chairman Gareth Davies and opening it brought all the same memories flooding back.

* * *

I'm very pleased the boys were able to see me play at a high level of club rugby and for Wales. I captained every club I played for, won ten international caps and was fortunate enough to lead my country on one occasion. My first tour for Wales was 1996 in Australia, playing in all the games except the two Tests. The first game was against Western Australia on the Waca, the famous cricket pitch in Perth. In the crowd was my dad, who had taken a ten-hour flight from Auckland just to see me.

I was lucky to have been selected for the tour at all because I had torn a muscle just before the team left. Mark Davies, the physio, was very good to me and promised that he would get me ready not only for the tour, but for the first match. I looked a sight in my playing kit. I had a cauliflower ear and had strapping on my elbow and thigh. It looked as if I had a wetsuit on. Nigel Davies, who still laughs about the way I looked, cross-kicked in the game and I scored a try. One of my boyhood heroes, Terry Cobner, now the manager of the Wales team, gave me a row for being out wide on the wing, but I didn't care. I was where the ball was and I scored!

I was pack leader for the second match, calling the lineouts in Welsh – something unheard of for a 'Gwenty'! The funny thing was it was only Emyr Lewis and Derwyn Jones in the team who could speak the language – everyone else had to learn the calls and numbers like a parrot! One time at a lineout, I shouted, 'Un, dau, tri, pedro' instead of pedwar, the correct

Welsh word for four, and the assistant coach, Allan Lewis, came running down out of the stand shouting, 'Kingsley, you are continually taking the mickey out of my language!' He still doesn't believe me that it was a genuine mistake.

Despite the disappointment of not playing in the two Tests against Australia, I still felt that I had played well on tour. On my return, I was chosen to represent Wales again, against the Barbarians, and Martyn Williams and I were chosen to play as flankers. We won the game quite easily 31-10.

Although I had enjoyed playing with freedom and confidence for Ebbw Vale, I found putting on the red jersey of Wales at times overwhelming. It was all a bit too much for me then, I was afraid to make mistakes. I remember one big game in the Five Nations Championship against England in Cardiff in 1997. We lost heavily and, deep down, I knew I hadn't played my best. The responsibility of wearing the red jersey is immense. Watching internationals when I was growing up, little did I think that I would be part of the Welsh team some years later. I dreamt so much of doing it, but didn't make the most of it, because I should have been more confident and believed in myself.

That game against England was the last at the old Cardiff Arms Park before it was demolished to make way for the Millennium Stadium. I think that I had got too caught up in the occasion rather than the match in hand. It was a great honour, but honour doesn't win matches. We were well beaten on the day by a good England side that included Jeremy Guscott, Will Carling and Rob Andrew. As it turned out, it was to be Carling's and Andrew's last game for England together with our own Jonathan Davies. There is always pressure in international matches, with the added pressure of playing against England, particularly at home. I was desperately trying to impress and, I think, looking back, that I also added too much personal pressure, which doesn't help.

As a player, you'll do anything to get a bit of extra competitive edge, either real or imagined. My lucky charm was an old pair of Kappa boots. When I wore them for my club Ebbw Vale, we kept winning, so I thought I had to wear them when I played for Wales. Reebok sponsored the national team at that time so I had to paint my old Kappa boots to look like Reebok ones. I also wore two pairs of socks for every game. It didn't matter what colour they were! I also used to do a silly forward roll that Richard Parks began to do when he ran on the field. I started convincing myself that I needed to do these little things as part of a build-up to the match.

I was made captain of Wales in South Africa in 1998. I got called into the squad from New Zealand, where I had been visiting my father, and handed the captaincy when Rob Howley was injured. In the famous Loftus Versfeld Stadium, we got well and truly hammered by 96-13. Springbok fullback Percy Montgomery, who later came to play in Newport, scored thirty-one points on his own. It was a difficult tour as several senior players had said in advance that they were unavailable for selection. A lot of replacement players were called up on the week of the big match to travel over to South Africa and, to be honest, the preparation was pretty poor against a team that had won seventeen Tests on the bounce. The Springboks at that time were outstanding and, unfortunately, we had a team of inexperienced players. It was really no contest.

Although a number of young players in that Welsh squad have gone on to do very well, that day we were up against a team that was too good. They had beaten England and Ireland by huge margins too. After the match somebody said, 'Just forget about it.' That made me angry and I told the players, 'Never forget this day. Wake up every morning ready for training, remember how good South Africa were and how hard we have to work to catch them up.' In the press conference afterwards no one believed coach Dennis John when he predicted that we would beat the Springboks within a year. As it happened, Wales beat South Africa 21-19 in a half-finished Millennium Stadium in June 1999.

I was selected to play for the Barbarians in 2000 and was fortunate enough to play alongside 'big' little brother the late, great Jonah Lomu. My dad had been his agent since 1994 and he had become a good friend and someone who instilled in me the confidence and belief that I was good enough to play international rugby. Here was the biggest star in the world telling me that I could do it! He was a humble, generous, positive man. On that Baa Baas tour, record point-scoring outside half Neil Jenkins was one of the party, and Jonah asked me if I could get Neil's autograph for him . Quite separately, Neil had asked me if I could get Jonah to sign something for him. The admiration and respect the one had for the other was incredible. They were also both extremely humble men. I ended up arranging a pool game between them in the hotel lobby so that they could meet. After that tour, they became firm friends.

* * *

Despite playing a couple of seasons for Gloucester, Worcester and Pontypridd, I realised that my best playing days were behind me. Naturally, because of my father's background in coaching rugby, I had thought that maybe some day I would follow in his footsteps. Acting on advice and encouragement from Mostyn Richards at the WRU, I did levels two, three and four of the coaching courses before I finished playing.

I joined Doncaster Knights as player coach in 2003, but, after a year, was invited by Philippe Saint-André, with whom I had played at Gloucester, to join him as forwards coach at Sale Sharks. It was much too big an opportunity to turn down. It was difficult to leave Doncaster, but the opportunity to work in the Premiership at the age of thirty-four, with the calibre of the squad they had, proved irresistible. Being in contact with players like Jason Robinson, Charlie Hodgson and Andrew Sheridan was a fantastic experience and a great learning curve. In my first season at Sale, we reached the semi-final of the Premiership and won the European Shield. In my second season, we won the Guinness Premiership. I thought coaching was pretty straightforward, but I hadn't properly taken into account the quality and contribution of the players I'd been working with! Coaching inexperienced young players is very enjoyable and rewarding, but it's much more difficult to get the wins.

Philippe Saint-André moved on to Toulon and I was put in charge of Sale Sharks for two years. Before he left, he asked if I would join him at Toulon if the opportunity arose. Sale agreed that I could move on, but wanted time to bring in a replacement. My initial plan was to have a few months off and then go to France, but I had a call from Howard Thomas, the Vice President of Russian Rugby, asking if I would be interested in going to coach their national team for a brief period. Up until then, I had worked continuously since the introduction of professional rugby as a player and coach and I had promised myself a break, but I couldn't turn down an invitation like that.

As things turned out, I was asked if I would become the head coach and national teams director for Russia and lead their team to the World Cup in 2011 in New Zealand. For a boy from Blaina to be in charge of a team from a country with a one hundred and forty-three million population was remarkable. I said, 'da' ... 'yes' in Russian!

I spent three remarkable years in the job, meeting people I would never have expected to meet and travelling to countries that I'd only read about. The worldwide passion for rugby is remarkable – it's not just Wales and the Welsh that are mad about the game. Russians are no different. This was a great life experience.

My family stayed at home because I had to travel so much. From Sochi on the Black Sea to scouting in Siberia or South Russia, I was constantly on the move. To ask my family to uproot to Russia and then for me to leave them for four months wouldn't have been fair, so I commuted. Being a long time away from my new young family was very hard and I missed my wife, Louisa, and three children, Gwenlili, Harmoni and the next generation Kingsley Jones.

I will never forget the time that Russia played Georgia in Tblisi in 2012. Just before the game, I was in a meeting in Sochi on the Black Sea and Tblisi is about a six-hour road journey south into Georgia. I suggested driving to the match and staying somewhere the night before. Everyone started laughing. They explained we had to fly, as driving into Georgia from the north could make us a target for terrorists. Instead, we would fly to Moscow, then to Armenia and come in from the south, as it would be safer. They said we would travel over the mountains and, being Welsh, I thought I was well prepared for that. I realised very quickly they were a bit bigger than Snowdon and we finally arrived at three o'clock in the morning. About a hundred journalists were waiting in a press conference to ask me politically loaded questions, as Russia had not played against Georgia in Tblisi for many years. Thankfully my translator dealt with all that for me.

Even before the match started, the anthem was drowned out and, during the game, every time Russia touched the ball all you could hear was whistling. It was a really hostile environment. There were thirty thousand spectators crammed inside the stadium and at least another ten thousand outside trying to get in. The noise was unbelievable. This was the ultimate challenge. It was terrifying.

On that same day when Russia played Georgia in 2012, Wales beat France to win the Grand Slam. I had spent a lot of time with Welsh hooker Matthew Rees and he rang me after the game to say thank you. He reminded me that I had told him that one day he would win fifty caps and in the game against France he had reached that milestone. I replied that I had only said that to him as I was fed up of him whingeing, and actually never thought he'd get even one! He laughed. Tblisi felt a very long way from home that day.

* * *

Early on in my time in Russia I realised that the teams there didn't have lots of big, strong prop forwards. They had lots of tall, fast players but the shorter, stronger men took up wrestling, as it is their national sport. The International Rugby Board asked me to go to Dagestan, an area notorious for terrorism and radicalising young people, to try to persuade the wrestlers who couldn't make the Russian national team to play rugby. We called it 'Project Prop'. It was one of the scariest things I have ever done in my life.

I was accompanied by the Minister for Sport, himself a former international wrestler, a convoy of five armoured cars, and fourteen armed guards during the whole trip. Every time the minister moved, they moved! The message of the trip was 'Rugby against terrorism'. It was like a scene out of old war footage with checkpoints and men in balaclavas. There were tanks in the road and road blocks everywhere. At airports, we were never stopped at passport control and were whisked away in cars straight off the runway like something out of a James Bond film. I was treated very well, but I didn't appreciate at the time the danger that I was in.

Project Prop worked and it was only when new recruits started playing rugby for the first time that I realised how important this initiative was. I gained a lot of respect from people in Russia for being part of that but, if I'm honest, I didn't realise how intense it was going to be – and my wife certainly didn't! When I left the country, the Minister presented me with a very expensive, beautiful, ivory tungsten sword and a Russian sheepskin hat. He shook my hand and told me I was a very brave man but, looking back, I wish I'd had more information before I took the job!

My father's words to me as a teenager were very important. He wanted me to make the most of all my opportunities. He encouraged me to take chances. He would say, 'When you look back in twenty years, will you think what *have* I done or what *should* I have done? It's too late then.'

I give similar advice to my two sons, Rhys and Dorian. I tell them humility is important. I don't believe the saying that nice guys don't succeed. Most of the great men I have worked with at the top level are the most humble people I know. I tell them to be confident in their own ability, but also to make sure they remember their roots. Rhys played for Wales under-18s at the age of sixteen against Ireland. Standing watching him singing the anthem was one of the proudest moments in my life, certainly more important to me than anything I have done. In 2014, Rhys and his brother Dorian played together for the Wales Sevens team against England at Twickenham. I carry a photo of the two of them playing together that day everywhere I go.

My rugby career has come full circle, and now I am back in Gwent as Head Coach to the Newport Gwent Dragons. My two older sons play rugby and maybe, one day, the younger Kingsley will follow in their footsteps. I hope, like my father, that I will always be supportive and wish them every success.

Some of my best friends have come through rugby. I can go to countries all over the world, walk into any rugby club and meet up with people who share my passion for the game. It's a sport that you can play at the highest level if you're good at it or, if not, just enjoy.

Rugby football is the greatest game in the world. Its popularity is amazing and it is now played in over a hundred countries. I am proud and privileged to be part of the global rugby family and I know that my father felt the same way. I hope my sons do too.

ACKNOWLEDGMENTS

Thank you to all the great players and sportsmen for their stories, wit and wisdom. You are the real heroes and inspiration to so many.

Thanks also to Angela Tillcock for her practical help and encouragement!

A sample from…

CAPTAIN COURAGE: GARETH THOMAS

Chapter One

'Gareth Thomas is a hundred percenter! He always gave a hundred per cent both in training and on match day.'

Jonathan Davies MBE,
Wales and British and Irish Lions,
Great Britain rugby league international

My first memory of rugby was the joy of just running with the ball in Bryncethin Junior School near Bridgend. It was fun and there was no pressure. But when I joined the comprehensive school, things were different. The school was so much bigger and you actually had to show you could play the game before you got into the team. For my first session, my mother had bought me rugby boots from Woolworths. Everybody else had Adidas or Nike rugby boots! I felt as if everyone was thinking, 'Well, he's not going to be any good with rugby boots from Woolworths!'

However, I remember being quite good in training

and learnt quickly that it's the quality of the person that matters, not the boots. I realised at a very young age how much I loved rugby and what the game of rugby meant to me. I enjoyed being part of a team and understood that while we were all different, we all had something to offer. For me, the game was about sharing skills and not about being a star because you were the speediest or the strongest on the pitch. I was always fast in school but I wasn't someone who was picked out as being special. Even though I loved the game, I was far from being the outstanding player in the team. I wasn't the one who could change the course of a game or do magic things to win a match. I wasn't even close to that. If I was selected to play, to me that seemed a massive achievement as I never felt I excelled as others did. I was picked as a substitute a lot of the time, and I was happy with that as it still gave me a role to play. Others might react badly to being put on the bench and have a strop or a sulk about it, but it never bothered me. I told myself that the team was what mattered.

My PE teacher at Ogmore School, Mr John, was my inspiration. Years later, I was touched to learn that he turned up regularly to watch me play for Bridgend but never made himself known to me. PE and Mr John were the only reasons I went to school. To know that he had seen me doing really well was very special to me. He was a typical sports teacher, willing to give hours and hours outside of school during the week and on Saturday mornings so that his teams did well. He was strict, with very clear boundaries for what he would and wouldn't accept from us on and off the pitch. He understood the boys who needed sport in school to let off steam. He made going to school bearable for me. He gave me a reason to go to classes. I don't think I would have gone if he hadn't been there. I would sit through eight lessons a day to be able to do one lesson of PE!

English was one other subject I liked. I was quite creative and I enjoyed reading plays but as a 'sporty' boy that didn't really fit in with my image. Everything else failed to inspire me so I was happy to leave school at sixteen. I knew I was never going to get A grades and that gave me the drive and ambition to go for the one thing I was good at – rugby. My parents knew that too and could see there was no point in forcing me to stay in school. I started my GCSE exams but I didn't want to complete them. It was horrible sitting an exam with very little to write, while everyone around me seemed to be filling in page after page. Lessons, exams and school were not for me.

My parents made it clear that I could leave, but only once I had found myself a job. So I went to the Job Centre with my mum the very day that I finished my exams and saw a job advertised in a local factory. The next day I started in Pressrite Engineering in Bridgend, making filters. It was the hardest job I have ever had in my life. I remember, at the end of that first day of work, I came home at five o'clock and said to my mother that I wanted to go upstairs for an hour before tea. I was absolutely shattered, went to bed and woke up the next morning still in my working clothes. I couldn't believe it. This was what real work was like!

I stayed at Pressrite Engineering for six or seven months until my father got me an apprenticeship as a postman like him. I moved up to earning £125 a week, which was a fortune to me! I really enjoyed working as a postman. I was becoming quite good at rugby by now and the job became like an extra sports session for me. I'd go on my round, carrying really heavy bags of letters and parcels and run the round as if I was training. I'd go to the gym straight afterwards and then go back to the post office for the second deliveries and run the routes again. After work, I'd go home, have a short sleep, and get up and go training at Pencoed Rugby Club in the evening. It was hard but it made me fit. I liked meeting people on my rounds and being out in the open air in my town, a place that meant the world to me.

I had the best time at Pencoed Rugby Club. It had a close-knit friendly community atmosphere and everyone looked out for one another. I learned my trade at the club. This was proper rugby. The sign outside the club said it all for me: 'Pencoed Rugby

Club – Delivering community rugby at its best'. I felt comfortable there and one of the boys when we chanted our team song:

'Who are… Who are… Who are we?

We are Pencoed RFC.

We don't swear. We don't fight.

We're the boys in red, blue, white.'

This was my world. I just loved being with my mates and putting all my energies into a sport that was my life.

I played for Pencoed until Bridgend signed me. I was thrilled when they did. Now I was able to play for a great club with a great rugby tradition. Players like J.P.R. Williams, J.J. Williams and Steve Fenwick had attracted huge crowds to the Brewery Field and had gone on to play for Wales and the British and Irish Lions. People used to say to my parents that I, too, was going to be a great player in the future and that they could see me playing for my country. It was nice to hear that but I was always more proud of compliments I got from people I played with. I looked up to more established players like Glen Webbe, the former Wales winger, and when he praised me it felt important and really meant something. I didn't get carried away, but it was encouraging.

This was a very happy time in my life. I was still a postman, even when I was playing for Bridgend. I was playing for the town where I had grown up and I was thrilled to be representing a place that I loved. In the week, I'd be out walking the streets and chatting to people who on a Saturday would be coming to watch me play rugby. I felt proud to be part of this community. I was their postman and their player and, to me, it was so much more than just a game of rugby. Rugby was the life and very soul of the town and when we beat the bigger clubs like Cardiff, Swansea or Neath it was brilliant, because it put Bridgend on top. I never genuinely thought I would play for Wales. I was just happy to have what I had always wanted, a life in sport. Lots of people along the way told me I had potential and said that, one day, I would play for my country. But I just thought people were being nice and I never took them seriously.

One day, Glen Webbe bet me a hundred pounds, a fortune to me then, that in the future I would play for Wales. I just laughed, but in 1995 I was selected for the Welsh squad to go to South Africa for the World Cup. The day I played for Wales he sent me a telegram saying, 'You owe me a hundred pounds.' He'd been right! The first thing I did when I got home from the tour was to go to see him and pay up on the bet. It was the best hundred pounds I ever paid out!

Chapter Two

'Gareth was a young inexperienced tourist at the 1995 World Cup but I recognised that he had the potential to be one of Wales' greatest players and he has achieved that honour.'

Robert Jones MBE, Wales and British and Irish Lions

One day my father collected the mail for our house at the sorting office to save the postman a delivery and he couldn't believe it when, in the middle of the parcels and bills, he saw a letter addressed to me with the magic letters WRU on the back of the envelope. I was sorting out my own post round and he raced straight over to where I was working. He stood next to me, waving the letter in excitement, saying, 'There's a letter from the Welsh Rugby Union!'

He wouldn't move from my side, waiting for me to tell him what was inside. I opened the letter and stared at it, unable quite to believe what was in front of me. I had been invited to join the squad training to go to the World Cup in South Africa in 1995. My father was so happy that I was being asked to join the huge Wales squad. I will never forget his face and how proud he was for me. My parents are the world to me and I was so glad that he was part of such a key moment in my life. I have always looked up to my parents and this moment was even more special because I knew what it meant to them, too.

I went to the World Cup, never expecting to play, but going there to train hard and to learn. The day before the team was announced, Steve Ford, the ex-winger from Cardiff, came up and congratulated me. I was confused until he told me that he wouldn't be playing and, therefore, I must have been chosen to play on the wing. I didn't believe him and thought that someone else was sure to be picked. I never thought it was possible that I might be on the list. When they announced the team the next day and my name was there, it was like a dream come true.

The jerseys were presented to us in the changing room the day before the game and I remember not knowing what to do with mine, as it was so precious. I'd heard stories of players who slept in their jerseys or who put them under their pillows all night. I had to think what would be best to inspire me and not just rely on what worked for others. So I hung my Welsh jersey in the most prominent place in my room where I could gaze at it all night. Then I took huge pride in putting it on, conscious of the three feathers placed over my heart. I filled up with pride and the determination to give my all. Just touching the badge of honour for my country inspired me. I thought proudly of all the players who had worn the Welsh jersey before me and what they must have been thinking as they received their shirts for the first time. This time, the honour was mine. It was up to me to do my best as other Welshmen had. Now that I had it in my possession, I had to do it justice and hold on it for as long as I could.

The pre-match speeches were very special and memorable to me. I listened carefully to the words of older, more experienced players and respected their thoughts on what it was like to win that first jersey and the advice they had chosen especially for that moment.

The first game I played for Wales, in a green jersey, was in the World Cup against Japan in the Free State Stadium in Bloemfontein, South Africa. I was one of two new caps that day, the other being Andy Moore, the Cardiff scrum half. It was an amazing debut for me as I scored a hat trick of tries and Wales won 57–10. Even then, I refused to take it all in and just kept telling myself that I had to keep working hard. I couldn't get carried away as the day wasn't about what I did, but about what the team achieved.

I remember hardly anything about the game as it all passed in a blur. People tell you to hold the moment but it all goes so quickly. I remember being proud to be part of a squad with greats like Mike Hall, Stuart Davies, Garin Jenkins and Robert Jones. These were the legends of Welsh rugby to me, the people I looked up to and wanted to be like. Throughout the tour I roomed with Robert, a most talented and highly-respected scrum half, and learnt so much from the way he coped under pressure. I wanted to be like that. He must have realised how naïve I was – I still talked about Bridgend all the time! But he and I got on really well because he took me under his wing. He showed me the ropes and helped me deal with fans and journalists. The whole tour was a whirlwind for me and, even though I was desperate to remember every detail, everything went by too quickly. I began to realise that these rugby heroes, my fellow teammates, were real people and not just stars who were cheered every match day. We were all proud to play our part and work together for each other and for Wales. We all understood what being selected to play for Wales meant and the responsibility we had to those who travelled far and wide to support us.

My next game was against New Zealand and I partnered Mike Hall in the centre, playing against the iconic Frank Bunce and Walter Little, considered by many to be one of the finest centre pairings ever to have played in the famous black jersey with the silver fern. I was nineteen years of age, scrawny, tall and up against the huge All Blacks team. Ellis Park in Johannesburg was the biggest stadium I had ever seen, able to hold sixty-thousand spectators, and it seemed as if each one of them was screaming at full voice. I looked around, completely in awe of my surroundings. It was humbling to stand in the tunnel side by side great rugby players like the New Zealand captain, Sean Fitzpatrick, and the giant Jonah Lomu, who was being called the sensation of the tournament. I remember thinking, 'What am I doing here? What is going to happen?' I had to keep telling myself that I deserved to be there. I tried hard to forget about the occasion, the atmosphere and the ground and to imagine that I was where I was happiest – the boy from Bridgend playing rugby on the Brewery Field. How lucky was I to have this chance to play against the best players in the world!

I learned so much that day. Even though we lost, it was one of the few times that Jonah Lomu failed to score – which was a source of great pride to me and my teammates. Just to be on the same field as the All Blacks was a great opportunity and I gave the game everything I had.

People ask what the haka can do to you before a big game. They ask: do you feel scared? Or do you try to front it up? And what do you think about? I can't remember facing the haka that day. I simply waited, lining up with the other Welsh players to accept the challenge. I could only concentrate on what was about to take place and keep my focus on what I had to do for the team. I was there ready to play for my country in the Welsh team. Despite the fearsome haka challenge of the All Blacks, I didn't worry about the star-studded team we were facing – it was the pride and passion of playing for Wales that inspired me in those last few minutes before kick-off. We started strongly and confidently and the Welsh flags were raised around the stadium, but this was a different match from my debut. We lost 34–9 against a much better team.

The next game, against Ireland, was a terrible one for us. We had to win to stay in the competition. I played on the wing that day but it was a game of rugby that never started. The team couldn't settle at all. The stadium was packed with Welsh and Irish supporters singing and cheering loudly. Celtic songs filled the stadium and 'Fields of Athenry' and 'Calon Lân' were sung with gusto and fervour to urge on the teams. Wales won the toss, but after that I can't remember touching the ball and I learned that things can change quickly and don't always go the way you want them to go. We lost by just one point, 24–23. Not to reach the quarterfinals was a huge disappointment for everyone. After the game, everyone was quiet. It was painful not to achieve the things we had trained so hard for and set out to do. The eighty minutes were over and we were out. The team atmosphere was dark and depressing. We were all aware of how much this meant to the Welsh fans who, like us, had travelled to South Africa with high expectations of getting through the group, at the very least. Everyone felt down as we returned home without the victory we had hoped for. For us, the dream of the World Cup was over.

A sample from…

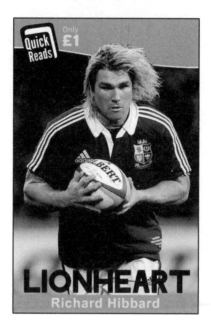

LIONHEART:
RICHARD HIBBARD

Chapter One

Growing Up

If it was ever going to happen, it would have happened then.

I had just helped the British and Irish Lions win a Test series in Australia, my tackle had crumpled their key player, and a picture of me celebrating with James Bond actor Daniel Craig, had been beamed around the world. It was my moment in the sun.

But it didn't happen that night, or the next. Just as it didn't happen after I won my first cap for Wales in 2006.

All my life I've been waiting for the phone to ring and for the bloke on the other end to tell me he was my dad. I don't know who he is or where he is. I don't know if he's still alive, or whether he even knows about me. The only certainty is that if the phone rang and he wanted to meet me, I'd agree.

After that, I don't know. A handshake … maybe an

awkward conversation. After which, I've no idea. Maybe I'd thump him for all the grief and struggle he'd caused Sibs. Who knows?

My mother never really talked about my father and I never really asked. Growing up, that's just the way it was. It wasn't discussed. Sometimes I used to imagine the phone at home might ring and he'd be on the other end, with some kind of explanation. But the call never came.

For the first few years of my life, I assumed my dad was the same guy as my brothers' dad. I can't remember exactly how the news was broken to me that, in fact, that wasn't the case. I think it was blurted out by one of my brothers during an argument. I'm told I have half-sisters through my dad, but I don't know anything about them and have never met them.

My wife, Louise, is probably more curious about my father than I am these days. I'm lucky that her dad is like a father to me. But I suppose I have always been seeking a father-figure in my life. I suppose I still am.

Sibs was my mum. Or Siriol Hibbard, to be precise. Me and my three brothers called her Sibs. My brothers' mates called her Sergeant Sibs because she was hard as nails and they were terrified of her.

I'm from Fairfield, one of the rougher areas in the middle of Port Talbot. It's near Aberavon Quins Rugby Club.

I lived opposite the comprehensive school, St

Joseph's. I was born in Neath Hospital in 1983 and I went to Sandfields Primary, which is in Fairfield.

I have three older brothers. Nicholas is the oldest, then Matthew, then Daniel. Nicholas is ten years older than me, Matthew (Ginger) is eight years older, and Daniel is six years older.

I was just a baby compared to those three. Nicholas had a different father from Matthew and Daniel. I had a different father again. My mother was married to Matthew and Daniel's dad, but they split up and she met someone else – my father.

But he was obviously a right beauty and didn't stick around after I came along, for whatever reason. So, growing up, it was just us five.

We lived at 25, Newton Avenue. About three years ago, Ginger bought the house back because we lost it at one stage. Mam had got in a mess with money and didn't pay any bills.

My mother died three years ago. But the good thing was that she'd moved back to that house before she died. She loved it there.

She died young at fifty-nine and very suddenly. There was no period of illness. She was diabetic and a big lady, but she rode a bike and seemed pretty healthy. Ginger was living with her, and one night he said she was feeling unwell. They took her into hospital and at 3 a.m. I had a phone call telling me I had better go there.

By the time I got there she had died – which was the worst part of it, the fact that I didn't get to see her.

It was tough because I'd had a brilliant pre-season and was in the best shape I'd been in for years. Her death knocked all that out of me. They were a difficult few months.

For two weeks after she died I would wake up at 3 a.m. every morning – the exact time I'd had the phone call. It wasn't a nice time.

My brothers were all rough, tough boys and my mother had to be pretty tough herself to put up with all of us. And they had their mates, some of whom were even worse.

We had a wall outside our house which got knocked down four times by joyriders, mostly mates of my brothers trying to show off. It was a well-known area for nicking cars.

Our house was a semi-detached, right next to all the prefab houses – or the 'tin houses' as we called them. You can see the school I lived opposite from the M4. Being so close to the motorway, sometimes we used to hit golf balls over it. The house had three bedrooms, but one of them was a box room. I shared with Ginge.

Ginge kept himself to himself, but could be a bit nutty every now and again. Daniel and Nicholas eventually ended up in the army.

One of my early memories is of Daniel and his mates trying to toughen me up by laying me on the floor and kicking me. They told me it was to make me harder. I remember one day I went punch for punch on the arm with one of Daniel's friends. I had a bruise on my arm the same size as the tattoo I've got there now. It was massive and my mother went nuts.

My mother protected me a lot from my brothers. Don't get me wrong – they didn't batter me or anything but I did get hit. Luckily I was big for my age – and I needed to be, to cope with those three.

Nick was big, Dan was stocky too, but Ginge was the runt of the litter. I got roughed up at an early age by them and that was pretty much how it went for the next few years.

My father's absence was something that simply wasn't discussed. Much later on, about five years ago, I sat Mam down and asked her a few questions about him but I didn't get many answers.

It was not as if my brothers saw much of their fathers, either, though. There wasn't really a father figure in our family, only my grandad who lived miles away in Haverfordwest.

My mother's mum was from Yorkshire and lived with my grandad in the house we lived in until she died and Grandad met someone from west Wales. So he gave Mam the house and moved down west. Now and again we would go and stay with Grandad.

The name Hibbard was Matthew and Daniel's dad's name. Jones was my mother's name, but I took her married name, even though I don't really have any connection with the Hibbard family, apart from through my brothers.

My mother used to work as a cleaner in one of the nightclubs in town. She used to take me along, which was good. It was called Wall Street, right in the town centre.

She also worked in play schemes for special-needs kids and used to take me along to those as well. We used to go on some good trips, especially in the summer.

Life was a struggle for my mum with four kids. She got into financial trouble a couple of times and we eventually lost the house.

I was about fourteen or fifteen at the time. We had to move, and ended up only two streets away, which was tough. Nick and Daniel had left by then, so there was just me, Ginge and Mam.

She didn't drive. If we ever went anywhere we used to go on bikes. In rain or shine, we'd go on our bikes – always. We were the bike family – that's how people knew us. That was a bit of a ball-ache, to be honest, but the only alternative was to walk everywhere.

We used to live on the corner at a T-junction. When the temperature dropped, and there was water on the road, cars would skid everywhere coming around the corner. Sometimes my brothers would try to make it smoother and more slippy. Fortunately, there were no real accidents – just people skidding and losing control.

I had a couple of mates who lived a few doors down. They got into a fair bit of trouble.

I also had two friends who lived around the corner. One ended up being a custody sergeant, booking people in at the police station. A lot of those he booked in were other mates of mine or kids who lived nearby!

I had another mate who was in foster care at one point and went off the rails. But he's doing well now as a welder. He was a clever boy, but they had to separate us in school because we were as thick as thieves for a while and got into a fair bit of trouble.

Sandfields Primary and Junior school were on the same site with a playground in between them. My brothers were renowned as tough boys, so their reputation followed me. It was a decent school, but the headmaster – Mr Pemberton – hated me, probably because I wasn't the nicest of kids. We had a few run-ins.

I remember he used to carry this big mobile phone around with him and he'd poke you with it – shove it right into your chest. I didn't like that. He was a right beaut, Mr Pemberton.

But I had some good teachers as well. I still keep in touch with Mr Dwyer even now. He was a good bloke – one of the few I got on with.

It was a fairly rough school with a bit of a reputation. But I suppose I must still like the area, because I've moved only five minutes down the road, where I live with Louise and our two daughters, Tiella and Summer. I don't think I'll ever leave Port Talbot. All my friends are here and I believe you should never forget where you're from.

My main friends are still non-rugby friends. I don't socialise much with rugby people – at least, not top-level rugby people. Most of my best mates still play rugby for Taibach.

I never really liked school. I think I had ADHD – attention deficit hyperactivity disorder – before it became a well-known condition. Nothing interested me or could keep my attention.

So I never worked at my studies. I was more interested in being Jack the Lad. I always wanted to be a rugby player. My ambition didn't change from primary school through to college.

My college teacher once asked me, "Rich, what are you doing here? You've got no interest in studying." I told him he was right. It was just a back-up plan in case I didn't make it as a rugby player.

I can remember playing only one rugby match for my primary school because I think that was all we had – one tournament played on Aberavon's Talbot Athletic Ground. But we won it and I remember it felt really good.

I lived in front of St Joseph's Comprehensive School, so at least we had playing fields to play on after primary school. But I didn't end up going to that school because I wasn't allowed in. The headmaster stopped me going there because every time he drove past I used to chuck spuds at his car. I did it as a wind-up. It didn't help my cause that my brothers had knocked the head off the school's statue of St Joseph and, every weekend, they'd also put a can of lager in his hand. If I'm honest, we plagued that school.

When we weren't on their fields playing rugby and football, we were on the school roof chucking stones. They also had an old water tower there which we used to climb. So, I went to Glan Afan Comprehensive School instead.

I had a happy childhood but money was very tight. One of my worst memories is sitting in Aberavon Quins Rugby Club after games as a kid and having no money to buy a can of Coke like all the other boys. I had to rely on their parents to buy me one because I had nothing in my pockets.

It was a horrible feeling and it's stayed with me. Earning decent money was one of the real drivers for me to make it as a professional rugby player. I can remember one day at school a professional rugby player came to help at a presentation. I can't remember who he was, or which team he played for. But it struck me that he drove a nice sponsored car, with big letters down the side, and something inside me twigged that I could be like that.

My mother came to only a handful of games because she thought rugby was too rough and she didn't like it when I got hurt.

I enjoyed playing rugby far more than watching it. I had no real favourite team or players who were heroes to me.

I liked Ieuan Evans, because he scored a try for Wales that beat England, but that was about it.

I never watched rugby. In my house, Ginge had control of the TV set and he only wanted to watch Star Trek.

My brothers weren't really into rugby, although Daniel did get a cap for the Boys Club of Wales. They went a different way to me. I can remember them sitting in Dan's room smoking and me thinking: I don't want to end up like that. There were plenty of opportunities, but I never really touched drugs.

I think my mother knew what they were up to in that room. But she probably took the view that it was safer for them to do it in her house than out on the streets.

I never really fancied taking dope, probably because it would have been so easy and no challenge. All I needed to do was walk into that room.

On Saturday nights, we used to sit on a wall outside and local boys would put a show on. By that I mean they'd nick cars and drive them up and down. Back then cars were just so easy to take.

We lived on a T-junction, so the cars would skid

around the corner and our own wall got hit regularly. We'd be sitting on the school wall opposite – crowds of us, watching. That's what passed for Saturday night entertainment in those days.

I never had a go at joyriding myself. I think it was the age gap – my brothers stopped me because they knew I was too young.

Most of those involved were about six years older than me. So I was the little kid who was allowed to watch, but that was it. Bigger boys would sit there, smoking and drinking, waiting for the next car to be driven past.

One night, a boy who had nicked a car wound down the window. "Keep hold of this," he said and handed over a doctor's bag. He'd actually nicked the doctor's car. We hid the bag in a garden. It was all a bit wild.

My brother Nick had a habit of getting drunk and then nicking things. Not stuff from shops, but random things like For Sale signs. One day, my mother woke up and there were about fifty For Sale signs in the house. Nick had been in competition with his mates to see who could collect the most.

He took carpets from the town centre and other stuff, and then one day he came back with a goat.

Nick was wild. He and his mates also made amazing bonfires in the park near our house. They would be so big they would melt the guttering on the houses fifty metres away. They would be collecting wood and tyres for months.

I never actually saw my brothers involved in the car stealing. I only remember them watching. You would see the occasional police car, but not many.

I always used to help Mam do the food shopping. We would get it home and it would then be a choice between eating it all straight away or letting my brothers eat it all straight away.

Mam wasn't the best cook in the world, which is maybe why I rarely suffer food poisoning, wherever I am. I developed an iron-clad stomach.

But my mother needed to eat well to keep her strength up. It allowed her to give us a few beatings if we got too much out of line. She was the only person I was ever really scared of. She wasn't called Sergeant Sibs for nothing.

Nicholas went into the army and Daniel followed him, so then there was just me, Mum, and Ginge. I still didn't get my own room, though, because Dan would claim it when he came home from the army.

Ginge was a tyre-fitter and he was the one who paid for us to have Sky. That gave him control of the only TV in the house, so it meant we watched endless episodes of Star Trek.

Chapter Two

Starting out in Rugby

I suppose I was about ten years old when I started to play organised rugby games down at Aberavon Quins.

I was a naturally aggressive sort of person and that dragged me through games when I was a boy. I knew I was a tough kid and I knew I was up against kids who weren't as tough.

Although I was looking for a father-figure, I think what I really wanted was someone to tell me I was doing OK. I had a bit of a difficulty with authority which caused me problems.

I was a prop in those days, but my interest in rugby wasn't really full on. It came and went and so did I.

I wasn't dedicated. I certainly didn't take training very seriously. Maybe I was avoiding the discipline and authority that a proper commitment might have meant.

I was about thirteen or fourteen when the Quins

junior section team I played for suddenly folded. So I went to play for Aberavon Green Stars, but that only lasted a year or so before they folded as well.

That took me to Taibach Rugby Club and it was there that I began to take the game seriously for the first time, at about the age of fourteen. It was difficult because it was quite a walk from my house and Mam didn't have a car.

But I was becoming a better player at school and playing for the older year group. That was giving me a bit more leeway at school with some teachers and made life a bit easier.

I had some decent teachers at that stage, like Mrs Protheroe, and they made me realise I could go one of two ways. I could hang out with the kids who spent all day nicking stuff from shops, or stay on a more acceptable course – certainly in the eyes of other boys' parents, who I was eager to be accepted by. I wanted people to like me.

Deep down I know I was a bit of a bully. My brothers had a reputation and being a tough kid myself it was easy to get my own way if I really wanted to.

At Glan Afan, I knew there weren't many other boys I needed to be scared of. I didn't get into too many fights, but I didn't need to. The family had a reputation, especially Daniel.

I did get into one fight – against a kid from another school who also had a reputation. It was almost an organised event, with other kids standing around watching. There were no words exchanged – just a stare and then we went to it, like a couple of ice-hockey players. It took me a while to get on top, but I think I won eventually, before it was broken up by some passers-by.

I played rugby against the same boy soon after and we ended up having another fight on the pitch. That time, he stormed off and told me he was going to get a knife. Fortunately, he didn't.

I can't say I enjoyed fighting. I wasn't scared of getting hurt, but I was scared of losing. It was a matter of pride.

I was aware that the parents of other boys at Taibach were a bit wary of me. They thought I was bad news even though I didn't really have many fights out on the field. It was a feeling I picked up, so I decided to try to keep myself in check and become more dedicated at rugby. I wanted people to accept me. I wanted to prove I wasn't trouble.

Taibach drew its players from a wider base than the Quins or the Green Stars. It was more like a Port Talbot-wide regional side. And we were good at that youth level. We almost won our league in the first year I was there and managed to win it in the second year without losing a game.

By my third year there, college teams had started to call on our players and the numbers dwindled. We weren't so successful that season, but the important thing for me was that youth rugby allowed me to take the sport seriously. It was well organised and training was rigorous.

By that stage I was even training on Christmas Day morning. I'd also run home from the club.

I went through most of the rugby club initiations at Taibach: first pint, first yard of ale, first tour with proper drinking. But drinking was never that important for me.

In fact, when I was seventeen or eighteen I stopped drinking altogether for a time. I still wanted to go out with my mates, though, so I began working as a bouncer at some of the bars in Port Talbot.

I was the tidy one, the nice guy, if you like. There were others who were less sympathetic to difficult customers. At one place I worked there was a puddle on the rough ground out the back. Some of the bouncers used to piss in it and if anyone caused any trouble they'd be dragged through that puddle before being sent on their way.

A fair bit of drugs were used by some of the guys I worked with. I remember one of them had to stop working because he was hearing voices.

We used to get paid £40 for the night and free Red Bull. I worked at a pub called the St Oswald's, then the Welcome To Town, then the Carlton. I enjoyed it but I made sure I was off the drink for the whole of that time.

At about eighteen, I had a best mate called Matthew Bradley. We were great friends and used to train together and go out together. That's when I began drinking again, because it was very hard in those days to be involved in a rugby club and not drink. It's much easier now for young players who are in academy environments, but in those days all rugby clubs either revolved around drinking or had a strong drinking culture. That was the way it was. So, although I had decided to try to take rugby seriously, when I stopped working as a doorman I went back to drinking.

My academic career at this stage wasn't much to write home about. I wasn't interested in school and couldn't find much to motivate me. I left school with a few GCSEs and then a GNVQ in business studies, but not much idea of what I wanted to do. In my last year at school I often wouldn't turn up until 11 a.m. but the teachers seemed to let me get away with it.

I had some ambition to be a fireman, so I went to Neath Port Talbot College, Afan Campus, to study public services. My other option was to follow my brothers into the army. But I didn't have my heart set on exams and things like that.

Aberavon were one of the main rugby clubs in Wales at the time, but I wasn't really interested in watching them. In fact, I had little interest in watching any rugby. I liked playing, and that was it.

For Taibach, we would train on Tuesday and Thursday nights. I was still carrying a bit of extra weight in those days, but nobody seemed to care. I also started playing for Baglan at youth level, which enabled me to play on Sundays as well as Saturdays. One day, though, Taibach played Baglan and I played for Taibach. The Baglan boys obviously didn't think much of that so they battered me. Their props, who were hard boys, took turns in holding me while the other punched me in the head. I was given a proper leathering.

I was capped by Wales Youth at Under-18 level as a prop and that's when it kicked in that I was doing OK at rugby. But although I was training hard there was still something missing from my development as a player. Then one day in youth rugby we met a guy called Phil White. He introduced us to weight training.

After my first weight session, I walked out of the gym and was immediately sick. I could hardly walk. There hadn't been any heavy lifting. It was more of a weights circuit, but my body wasn't used to it and I found it hard.

I got better, though. But I noticed other boys started to drop by the wayside. Eventually, although the whole Taibach Youth team had started with him, it came down to just me and Phil. I became hooked and I'd be phoning him up asking when the next session was. I'd plague him.

I was definitely feeling the benefits of the weights and I was also getting my overall fitness up by running to the gym and then back to the house.

Eventually, I ended up working for Phil in his window company, so he was a good influence in more ways then one.

After getting my cap at eighteen, I stepped up the weights even more and began to lose a lot of weight. I even moved from prop to the back row.

I knew I was improving, but some things weren't quite what I expected, or even enjoyed.

That Wales Youth cap – which I gained out in Italy in 2003 – proved to be my one and only. I had gone out there carrying a shoulder injury, mainly due to my own stupidity. I had played too many games in the build-up for no other reason than I couldn't say no to teams when they asked.

I liked Taibach and Baglan but Wales Youth was unfamiliar territory for me. It was all different – new team-mates, new coaches, new ways of doing things. I didn't like change. I liked things I knew, things that had become familiar.

It was also a big deal for me just going to Italy. I hadn't travelled much before that and I couldn't afford to take any spending money.

Some of the bigger clubs were now taking notice of me, but I had no means of travelling to see them. I could hardly go those distances on my bike!

Bridgend were keen on me and I went to a few of their training sessions, thanks to the father of a friend who took me in his car. I suppose I should have explained to these clubs that we didn't have a car in our family, but I never did. It wasn't that I was too shy or embarrassed to explain. I just didn't like talking to people. I was anti-social – still am, in many ways.

In my second year of youth rugby, Swansea asked me to go and play for their Under-21 Academy side.

I played a few matches for them, but the club was having terrible financial problems at that time. It was a strange period, because I went straight from youth rugby to playing one match in 2003 for the senior Swansea side against Pontypridd at Sardis Road.

Matthew, my mate, ended up playing three games for the senior team, but I hesitated because I'd started doing something completely out of character for me, something I'm amazed about now when I think back. I'd started watching a little bit of rugby league on TV, and thought it looked exciting. I also felt it suited my style of rugby. So, without any prompting, I decided to email all the rugby league clubs in the north and ask them for a trial.

I had loads of replies. A few said they were interested and one of those was St Helens, who had a contact in Aberavon that they sounded out.

They asked me up for a trial and I stayed there for three weeks. I played in games against Wakefield,

Salford and Leeds for the Saints Academy team.

Looking back, I think I turned to rugby league as a result of the Wales Youth appearance not going as well as I had hoped. I felt I'd missed an opportunity, so I looked around for another option.

But I enjoyed my little spell in the north. I stayed in a house with Ade Gardner, the wing who went on to have a great career with Saints and played for Great Britain.

The training was different from rugby union training and I enjoyed it. I didn't know all the rules, but I got by and felt I did OK. St Helens also thought I did OK, but they didn't rush to push a contract under my nose, so I expect they had other possible signings. It also didn't help their interest in me that soon after I came back home I tore ligaments in my ankle.

But I came back with a liking for rugby league, and decided to play for a team that had been created back home, called Aberavon Fighting Irish.

It was a summer league, so I could play rugby union in the winter and switch to rugby league when the union season ended in May.

It was a great crack. Our coach was Chris O'Callaghan, who was a real character. He had coached rugby union at Aberavon. It meant we had a lot of the Aberavon boys playing for the Fighting Irish in the summer.

They took their name from the Aberavon Green

Stars and the Irish links with that club. They were crazy – but great fun.

I played that first summer in 2003 and then carried on for a few years after, even though I wasn't officially allowed to. I had to be a bit secretive about my days with the Fighting Irish, so I played under the registered name of Hubert Richards. It was the team manager who dreamed that up. What a genius. Richard Hibbard disguised as Hubert Richards.

I got away with it by the skin of my teeth. I signed for the Ospreys later on and if they had found out I would have been in some serious trouble.

In rugby league I used to play loose forward and loved it. Everything that I really enjoy about rugby union – carrying the ball and smashing into people – you get to do over and over again in rugby league.

I sometimes wonder what might have happened if I'd been offered a deal by St Helens. Maybe I wouldn't have grasped it – because Keiron Cunningham was there at the time – but it's something I've day-dreamed about, playing with Sean Long and all the rest of their great players.

Whether it was risky or not – and whether Swansea and the Ospreys turned a blind eye to it or not – my rugby league summers were definitely helpful. They got me really fit each summer and hardened me up.

By the summer of 2003, I had begun pre-season training with Swansea but there was a great deal of change within the game at that time and regional rugby had arrived.

The Ospreys had been formed from a merger between Swansea and Neath, although both clubs carried on operating club sides under their traditional names in the new Welsh Premiership, below the new regional level.

I played thirty-one matches for Swansea in that 2003–04 season and it was during that time that I was converted from a prop who could also play back row, into a hooker.

Basically the game was changing, and taller players were dominating the back row positions. I was told I could either become an average back row forward or a good hooker. It was an easy choice when they put it like that.

My coaches during that time with Swansea were Keith Colclough and Tony Clement – both great guys and very good coaches.

It was a turbulent time at the club after the creation of the Ospreys. People were still feeling their way. But it was nothing compared to the turbulence created by my attempts to turn myself into a hooker!

It meant learning to throw the ball into the line-out and I was shocking, truly terrible. It was a tough learning period and it would take me four years, and about fifty different throwing techniques, before I really got it right.

I had practised a lot before my first game as hooker, but that didn't stop the whole thing being a nightmare.

Chris Wells, the Ospreys hooker at the time, helped me out. I needed a lot of help. When I threw into the line-out, the ball could literally go anywhere.

In one early game as hooker, I was so bad that my throw didn't even reach the line-out because it struck the back of a prop's head. The touch judge must have felt sorry for me because he let me pick it up and throw it in again!

The idea that I could ever do this for my country, at international level, seemed a million miles away.

A sample from…

THE HARDEST TEST:
SCOTT QUINNELL

Chapter One

The morning of 21st November 2000 should have been the happiest moment of my rugby career. We were preparing to face South Africa at the Millennium Stadium the following Saturday. As I was eating breakfast, Graham Henry, the Welsh coach, came over to talk to me. An injury had ruled out stand-in captain Mark Taylor and he was offering me the Welsh captaincy for the first time.

I was very honoured and obviously happy. To captain your country is the pinnacle of any player's career. But the more I thought about it and what the responsibility entailed, the more I began to worry.

For the week leading up to the match, I hardly slept. Believe me, it had nothing to do with captaining Wales in front of 72,000 people, nor indeed anything to do with rugby at all. What absolutely petrified me was the prospect of having to speak in front of the players, their families and dignitaries after the game. That was it, nothing more.

My mind would go back to being eighteen again when I was asked to open a fête in my old primary school and the fear that had triggered. Then, too, I hardly slept during the nights leading up to the event. It might seem crazy – I only had to say "I declare this fête open". It must seem surprising that something so easy could cause me such anxiety, but my experiences up to that point had left me with little or no confidence when it came to such things.

There's a picture of me when I'm very young at primary school wearing a red rugby jersey. I think it must be one of my dad's, because it's drowning me, but I look very happy. And yet at that time I had no idea what rugby was, let alone how much of a role it would play in the rest of my life. It makes me smile just to look at it.

I started school aged four. Five Roads Junior School was barely 300 yards from where we lived and was very much part of the small village where I grew up.

Learning at that age is all about fun and you soon forget about being left at school every day by your parents. To me, it was just somewhere else to spend time with the friends who were so much a part of my life outside school. That's what made things easier, I guess – we grew up discovering new things together and it was like one big family.

Everywhere there were familiar faces. I recognised

the teachers from around the village and even the dinner lady was my best friend Martin's mother – her cawl was one reason for anyone to want to go to school!

You hear of schools struggling these days with large classes; at Five Roads we benefited from the extra attention that being in small school groups allows.

Thinking back, and with what I know now, I must have shown early signs of learning difficulties. But I don't think there was anything particularly different about me. I was quite a confident kid, eager to have a go at anything.

I remember vividly being given the responsibility of being milk monitor, a job I took to with relish – my proudest moment up 'til then, with the added incentive of being able to have an extra bottle now and again!

Five Roads was and still is very much a close-knit community; everyone knew each other's families and it was safe for us kids to play out until all hours.

Regular events like the carnival brought the community even closer together. I've a vivid memory of one such carnival enjoyed by myself, my friend Martin and my younger brother Craig. We all dressed as rugby players and insisted on walking round all day in those thick, cotton jerseys in the sweltering summer heat, getting up to no good in Mervyn Davies-style headbands. Craig and I had little idea that in the years to come we'd be spending quite a lot of time running around in kit – though I must say I've not been tempted to adopt my godfather Mervyn's 'John McEnroe' look any time since.

The move from primary up to secondary school is enormous for any child. It's gut-wrenching to be separated from the friends you've grown up with and to move away from the security of a school where the teachers know you almost as well as your parents. Leaving Five Roads School was no different – and I really wasn't prepared for the struggle that secondary school would bring.

Chapter Two

My next school was Graig Comprehensive School down in Llanelli itself. I used to catch the bus from the village square just outside The Stag's Head with my friends each morning but, instead of spending all day together, as soon as we got to school we'd all have to go in our different directions.

Arriving at secondary school can be an isolating as well as a daunting experience – for a start it's the first time in your life your academic ability is truly measured, and by being put into streams or sets you get labelled. I found this particularly difficult.

I've always liked the idea of learning and, looking back, I think how great it would have been to be one of those people who could devour all the new information. Unfortunately, I just couldn't. My poor concentration made this impossible.

I was keen to make an impression, but it wasn't long before I began to fall behind. It was very hard to deal with the fact that while my friends were doing well I was slipping to the bottom of the class. I couldn't understand why, even though I was trying all I could to keep up, I still kept falling further behind.

I tended to keep myself to myself in classes, not wanting to attract attention to the fact that I was struggling. I'd sit at the back waiting for the moment when the bell would ring and I'd be back out in the yard with my mates, where once again I could get involved.

The teachers tried everything to help – looking back I realise how frustrating it must have been for them to work with me, one week, to the point where I seemed to grasp some aspect of a subject, only to see me return the following week with little or no idea of what we'd gone through previously.

I was to learn later that this inability to retain information is one of the key signs of a learning disorder like dyslexia. My short attention span meant that much of the lessons was spent staring out of the window, daydreaming or counting the bricks of the building opposite. Maths was the only subject I grasped to any extent. In others I just kept repeating the same mistakes over and over again.

I'd find things like copying text from a blackboard very difficult. I now know that it was my dyslexia which caused my eyes to jump around the board or the page of a book, meaning I'd miss sentences. This meant having to read things several times, so I was much slower than everyone else at completing the tasks.

One of the major things I remember is feeling sick at the thought of being asked to read out loud. It terrified me – all the more reason to keep a low profile. Some teachers shouted at me, calling me lazy, and the constant rows upset me very much.

It is important to understand that back then little was known about learning difficulties. I really don't blame the teachers – I guess they had exhausted every method they knew, to little reward. But I couldn't understand why I was being punished. Slowly I began to realise I had problems of some sort. The fact that the other children seemed to move on easily left me feeling very alone. Soon, I was bottom of every class – that's if I was in the class at all!

My wife Nicola remembers finding a box full of my school books from this time when we moved in together, all the pages empty save for the date and the title. That about sums it up, I guess.

My parents began to realise that things weren't going well. There were the concerns of teachers in the form of reports and letters in the post. I'd often get home from school in tears and lock myself in my bedroom. They found it hard to understand why their eldest son, who had been so full of confidence, was becoming increasingly withdrawn. I used to ask to go to friends' birthday parties, only to quickly change my mind when we arrived, and have to be dragged in by my mother, and then leave soon after. My learning difficulties were now affecting every aspect of my life.

At fourteen my problems were getting out of control. I'd get increasingly frustrated with myself and got into a fair bit of trouble – if I could get kicked out of a lesson or miss one completely, all the better. I once even punched a friend after a minor argument, breaking his eye-socket in the process. Something had to give.

Despite all this, my parents were brilliant, spending lots time with me while I was doing my homework and trying different tutors to help me along. They looked at every possibility. When they saw that their efforts produced little improvement in school they started questioning themselves, as well as the credibility of the (very many) tutors in the Llanelli area who were assigned the huge challenge of improving my grades!

As my father has since said, "We knew he wasn't twp or dull, but it was frustrating."

I was pretty sharp when it came to things like sport but a complete failure academically.

Eventually my parents came to what I suppose, looking back, was a natural conclusion – that it was the sport, particularly the rugby (which I had by that time begun to get heavily involved in) which was to blame.

They imposed the ultimate penalty on me, stopping me playing rugby at Under 15 level – it turned out to be the only level I didn't play at.

I was devastated. By this time, rugby was all I really wanted to do and although I saw the importance of education I found it impossible. Everything seemed to be against me.

Thank goodness the ban didn't last for long!

Chapter Three

What's in a name? I was born Leon Scott Quinnell on August 20th 1972 in Morriston Hospital, Swansea – the wrong side of Loughor bridge as far as my family and future was concerned (though I'm told I was quickly rushed over to the Llanelli side in order to take my first breath!).

My father Derek had been a three-times British Lion as well as a Welsh international, and he had the honour of being the only player in the Lions squad not to have already been capped by his country when he went on the tour to New Zealand in 1971. My uncle is Wales and Lions legend Barry John and my godfather Mervyn Davies also pulled on both the Wales and Lions jerseys. (No pressure on me then, whilst growing up, to pick up the oval ball!)

Rugby did seem to be everywhere, even with my mother – she'd become a massive fan of the game after years of following her brother, Barry, and of course my father. My two youngest brothers, Craig and Gavin, followed us into the game as well, becoming professionals in their own right. So it's not hard to imagine what the topic of conversation was around the dinner table when we were growing up!

At the age of eight, I began showing an interest in the game which would eventually become my life. I asked my father to take me down to Stradey Park, Llanelli, to play for the U11s.

It might sound surprising, but up to then I hadn't really sat down to watch a game of rugby, not even to watch my father. I know now that my learning difficulties meant I didn't have the attention span to watch a whole match. In honesty I'm still not one for watching the game, though watching the game is now what pays the bills!

I recall my father being away a lot playing rugby when we were young. In 1977 he was on tour in New Zealand for three and a half months and again in South Africa for the same amount of time in 1980.

As well as our good friends in Five Roads, we were lucky to have Nan and Granddad next door to us, which must have really been a help for my mother when Dad was away. It was great to have an extended family right there. My grandfather Stan would spend hours with us as kids. I loved it when he helped me make bows and arrows and, later, encouraged me to drive diggers and tractors. What more could a boy want?

While on tour, my father was only allowed one phone call home a week and whenever I got to speak to him I spent the whole time in tears. In the end my mother decided that she would relay messages between us – a lot less trauma all round!

It had been Mr Rees, a lovely teacher at Five Roads School (who went on to teach both my daughters, Samantha and Lucy), who initially planted the rugby seed. He was the first guy to actually encourage me to pick up a rugby ball, taking us all training.

Although Dad must have been quite pleased when I showed an interest in the game, it's important to say that he never pressured me to follow in his footsteps. He was more than happy for me to make my own way in the world.

People often ask me about my hopes for my son Steele. I think they expect me to say that I'm longing for him to follow in my footsteps. That couldn't be further from the truth. I may be proved wrong but I think Steele is more likely to paint a game of rugby or write about it than play in it, and so be it! As I've learnt from my father, all you can do is let children follow their own paths in life.

Being on the rugby field brought on an instant change in me. Failure to deal with school had made me more and more withdrawn, but having the ball in my hands, caked in mud, seemed to bring out the real Scott. I felt in control for once and at last began to feel the rewards of effort and practice which had yielded so little at school.

At other times I could be found on my bike on the hills around Five Roads or playing cricket or football with friends: anything as long as it was sport, exercise and fun. The more involved I was in sporting activities, the more my confidence grew.

Later the family moved down to Pen-y-fai Lane, and the new house had the advantage of being near to town, and overlooking Stradey Park. I began to take a real interest in watching Llanelli play, and I was also now nearer to the weights gym and the squash courts. It was in these places I began to spend much of my time.

I've learnt that people with learning difficulties develop what they call "coping strategies" to deal with their condition. It usually means involving yourself in things that you are good at and not exposing yourself to unfamiliar situations, I guess it's because of fear of failure.

As books and writing and general academic work became more difficult for me, I began to spend more and more time on the rugby field or watching the game and, later, working out in the gym. It was where I felt comfortable, where I felt a real sense of belonging.

I still see that sense of camaraderie as rugby's

ultimate appeal. Wherever I've been in the world through rugby I've always felt a part of a family. This was no different in the early days.

As I made progress in the game, I started to feel sure that it was what I wanted to do for the rest of my life. After a few games representing the school, I was made captain, which was a massive honour for me. I also began playing for Llanelli schoolboys and went on to captain the Under 16s on tour to St Helens – my first ever trip away from my parents and a truly memorable occasion.

Whilst there I got to meet former Llanelli great Roy Mathias and also Stuart Evans (whom my dad had coached for a time with Wales). At sixteen I was 6' 1" and a bit of a lump but Stuart literally had to come through the door sideways to meet us! It was incredible – he's one of the biggest men I've ever come across in the game!

On the Sunday we got to see St Helens play at Knowsley Road and I was able to witness for the first time the wonderful sense of occasion that is part and parcel of the 13-man game.

After the match I was taken to meet the Saints' board, who out of the blue offered me a place in their academy set-up. I found it hard to believe what I was hearing. It was an incredible compliment and of course a real boost to my still fragile confidence.

But I felt very much that I wanted to make my mark in rugby union, and at that time my only wish was to play for the Llanelli first team. Everything else could wait.

Back at home, things were much the same. I began to miss school regularly, Wednesday afternoons in particular, which I would spend training. I recall one teacher cornering me one day and saying, "Quinnell, you'll never come to anything playing rugby, boy!"

His advice had come far too late for me!

I began to show even more dedication to the game. I d recently had a major eye-opener and a narrow escape, just missing out after a Welsh Under 15 trial, where I played at prop! I'd put on weight and was never so glad to have a hammering in my life! I realised if I was to get away from the dreaded front row and have a future in the game, I really had to focus.

Thinking about it, my negative experiences in school may have made me even more determined to prove myself. I wouldn't say I was a natural, but I was fortunate to have inherited a physique which, with work, helped me ply my trade in the No. 8 position.

Playing for Llanelli youth at sixteen, week in week out, against older boys of eighteen and nineteen really served to toughen me up and get me into shape. Believe me, you take some big knocks, but if you want it badly enough, you're always there the next week, ready for the next bout!

My career was moving at quite a pace and I had little time to stop and think about education and the problems of the past. Besides, I had found something rewarding. I felt useful at last.

I wonder sometimes whether or not that teacher has followed my career – I haven't bumped into him since!

Chapter Four

By the time I was seventeen I had more or less given up going to school. My time now was split between rugby and working for my dad as a representative in the family company. But somehow my father managed to persuade Graig headmaster Dennis Jones to allow me to stay enrolled in school. I had to re-sit maths in order to remain eligible to compete for a Wales Under 18 cap as well as work part-time for Dad. The re-sit was a minor diversion, keeping me in school longer than I'd anticipated – but I was prepared to do anything to pull on that Welsh jersey! I'd turn up at Graig in my Escort 1.4 company car (yes, I was a boy racer too!) wearing my school tie and leave later having changed into my work clothes and tie.

That Welsh U18 trial soon came around. It was held at Aberavon's Talbot Athletic Ground and was a huge moment in my life. I began the match in the "possibles" team, the mission being to play my way into "probables" for the second half. I was really determined to take this opportunity to show what I could offer. And sure enough, at half time, I was told to change sides for the rest of the game and to carry on where I'd left off, this time in the colours of the "probables".

Next it was back into the clubhouse for sausage and chips and the longest two-hour wait of my life. When the announcement finally came and my name was read out, it was like all my Christmases and birthdays had come at once. I was to pull on the cherished Welsh jersey against the Scots.

Memorably, I played for the Welsh Under 18s team against the Welsh Youth at Stradey Park. It was not memorable because we beat our senior opponents, but because the Youth team that day contained a certain Neil Jenkins and Scott Gibbs. That result would supply valuable ammunition for the future!

Then I was off to New Zealand with the school team, where we became one of the only sides (junior or senior) ever to win all six tour matches. This was no mean feat in the land where they live and breathe rugby almost as much as we Welsh!

The fact that I went on to miss my final maths exam, because I was conducting a different kind of maths involving my father's company and a business deal in Swansea, shows where my priorities now lay. I was chasing a different dream entirely! I didn't have time to feel that bad.

Not that my father had gained a top class employee. Working for him showed how my learning difficulties affected my life in the real world, as it had done at school. All employees were required to fill out call sheets and time sheets. When it was time for mine to be given in, I usually made some excuse, like I'd left them in the back of the car. My father's secretary Sue was probably the only reason I managed to keep on top of things. She would help me fill out the order forms at the end of each day and make sure everything was in order.

The highlight of my time with the Welsh Youth came in a match against England in Blackpool, where I somehow managed to score four tries in a big win. On the opposite side that day was one Lawrence Dallaglio. Thinking back, I wish I'd made a bit more of that victory. Managing to get one over on 'Lol' in a Welsh jersey only happened on one other occasion, on a famous sunny day in 1999 – but more of that later. I guess I peaked too early!

1990 was a very busy year for me. I represented Wales in Canada at Under 19 level and played for Wales at Youth level.

Then came my big chance. Llanelli were looking for youth players to join members of the first and second teams to play away at Penygroes in their centenary match.

I was given the nod. I cannot describe how great it felt to pull on the jersey for Llanelli for the first time. Remember, I had turned down an invitation to play league at St Helens just for this moment. I was following in my father's footsteps and representing the place that I loved. I really don't remember who won that day, but it didn't matter. I had worn that famous scarlet jersey. I prayed that this was to be the first of many occasions that I'd have that honour.

Chapter Five

The following season, 1991/92, brought with it another big opportunity. Llanelli's success domestically meant a number of our big name players, such as Lawrence Delaney, Phil May, Phil Davies, Emyr Lewis, Rupert Moon and Tony Copsey, would be away serving Wales in the World Cup. I was invited up to the first team. This was it. It was the massive opportunity that I'd been waiting for.

As well as myself, players such as Paul Jones, Huw Harries and Mathew Wintle, who had toured Canada with me at Wales Youth level, were also called up. On top of that, Allan Lewis, who was now coaching at Llanelli as Gareth Jenkins's no. 2, had been our coach at Wales Under 19s level. This all meant that even though I was moving on to a new, massive challenge, I had people around me I was familiar with. This helped a lot.

In the October of 1991 I met my future wife Nicola in a Llanelli pub one evening. I knew instantly she was the one. I recall very early in the relationship being on Llanelli beach together when Nicola began showing me over and over the correct way to pass a rugby ball (her dad Bryn coached Bynea Rugby at the time). I was bemused but said nothing.

A few days later she rang me after seeing my picture in the local paper. In one of the most surreal conversations I've ever had, she told me, "You play rugby for Llanelli!" To which I replied, "I know. Where do you think I go every Monday, Wednesday, Thursday and Saturday?" She said, "Oh well, I thought you just worked out in the gym like my brothers!" That's what I love about Nicola – she's never really been a rugby fan. She used to watch me play firstly for the social life and secondly to see that I didn't get hurt. It was a good thing I always drove home!

We soon moved in together and it was not long before we had our first child, Samantha. It was a wonderful time, like a whirlwind: I didn't want it to stop. I was still working for my father, which helped make ends meet in those pre-professional days but between that and training and playing at the weekend, I found I had little time left to spend with my new family.

I'll always remember seeing my first live Cup Final. It was 1985 and Gary Pearce converted a late drop goal to beat Cardiff and win the Cup for Llanelli. It sent real shivers down my spine. The whole of Llanelli seemed to be in Cardiff that day and being there was superb.

And to think that by the end of that busy 91/92 season, I myself was lining up in a Cup Final singing the National Anthem along with players such as Phil May, Ieuan Evans, Rupert Moon, Mark Perigo and Ricky Evans!

What a moment it was, knowing my friends and family were there in that massive crowd. We went on to defeat deadly rivals Swansea 16– 7 that day, which topped things off nicely!

You often hear of sports men and women having superstitions when preparing for a game. For instance, they may put their kit on in a certain order or listen to a certain song to get "psyched-up". It was around the time of that Cup Final that my lucky underpants entered my life.

I had worn these pants when playing all season. I'd developed a close bond with them, so much so that the thought of appearing in a match without them was unbearable.

On the day of the final my wife Nicola, mother, father and brother Craig had gone down to Stradey to catch the bus to Cardiff, as is the tradition for our supporters.

I was left at home to finalise my preparation and pack ready for the big match. I loaded my kit-bag as usual, but to my horror my lucky pants were nowhere to be seen! I decided quickly that either my father or Craig must have put them on. I rushed down to Stradey with a spare pair to catch the bus before it left. Luckily it was still there, so I boarded and demanded to see what pants they were wearing. It turned out to be Craig who was the villain of the piece. I quickly made him change into the spare pair and headed off to the final safe in the knowledge my lucky charm was in my bag. I'm certain we would have lost that day otherwise!

Playing rugby regularly for my beloved Llanelli in the shadows of the same saucepans on top of the posts that had beckoned my father was a great feeling. Even if the journey distance was much the same to Stradey Park as it had been to Graig (they are barely a mile apart), emotionally and psychologically I had come a long way.

Dad was always around, ready to give me advice on the game and I was never short of role models to look up to in the shape of his former colleagues and team mates who'd become close family friends over the years.

Being born into what's been called a "rugby dynasty" (a term that makes me cringe) didn't automatically mean my transition into the game was easy. As rugby became increasingly part of my life I quickly learnt that having a name like Quinnell had its negative aspects as well as positive ones.

Some people liked to assume I was only in the Llanelli side because of my name. I sometimes got into scrapes of an evening in town after a match and a couple of pints. After all, I was still a teenager at this time. And I'd be the first to admit I wasn't always in the right. But you're always going to have that in a small town, I guess. I was a big boy, too, and there are always people who want to have a pop to prove a point. But I learnt to avoid certain situations and environments. I began to realise that I needed to sacrifice some things in my life to get on in the game. Fortunately Nicola proved to be a calming influence on me too. We met at the right time.

It was a similar story on the field. I recall one cup match, when we were due to play Furnace United. Sometime the day before one of the boys had heard that the Furnace players had each put £10 in a pot to be taken by the first man who could get me off the field (presumably on a stretcher) in the game. I was used to the fact that I was becoming something of a scalp, but found this particularly underhanded and decided that even though I was tired (I'd played the night before for Wales Schools against France) I would now definitely play a full game. There was no way on earth I'd leave the field and give anyone the satisfaction (and the £150 quid!). Needless to say, the match was a bloody affair and when the ref blew up I was exhausted, black and blue but more than happy to have lasted the eighty minutes.

The Furnace boys were understandably a bit miffed and not entirely pleased when on our way back through the tunnel I suggested that, having lasted out, the money in the pot was rightfully mine! Of course, I didn't see any of it.

For more information about **Jos Andrews**

and other **Accent Press** titles

please visit

www.accentpress.co.uk

26/12/16